NORFOLK COUNTY VIRGINIA

EXTANT POOR HOUSE RECORDS

Sharon Rea Gable

Heritage Books
2023

HERITAGE BOOKS
AN IMPRINT OF HERITAGE BOOKS, INC.

Books, CDs, and more—Worldwide

For our listing of thousands of titles see our website
at
www.HeritageBooks.com

Published 2023 by
HERITAGE BOOKS, INC.
Publishing Division
5810 Ruatan Street
Berwyn Heights, MD 20740

Cover photo is courtesy of the Library of Virginia

International Standard Book Number
Paperbound: 978-0-7884-2965-1

PREFACE

The old Norfolk County poor house records housed in the Annex or State Records Center for the Library of Virginia consists of pages in a few ledger books, odd pieces of paper in varying sizes and numerous small pieces approximately 3 inches by 2 inches. They used these small pieces when they gave money to the poor to get their signature (usually a mark such as an X) indicating that they received the money and it also had the signature of the witness.

The information we used came from two groups all housed together – (1) Norfolk County/ Chesapeake Miscellaneous Power of Attorney 1745-1911 Overseer of the Poor 1786-188? Unprocessed 1745-1913 Box Number 1 and (2) Norfolk County Poor Records 1794 to 1801, deed 1786, Acc. No. 23707, Duke University Transfer.

These records seem to concentrate in 1790s through early 1800s with one as late as 1888. The book is arranged by date, but the date is in general terms only. Getting the odd pieces of paper in chronological order serves no purpose and wasn't attempted. For example the 1786 was an easy one as it only had one piece of paper which survived, but the next group is labeled 1793 through 1794 as the year for poor house records started on 1 April as per the Code of Virginia, Chapter 51 which you will see mentioned in a number of these pages and ended on 31 March. The custom of caring for the poor obviously started with our English ancestors and the early records were considered Church Warden records. The records in this book are after that period.

In 1761, Norfolk County was divided into 3 parishes (Portsmouth, St. Brides and the Elizabeth River Parish). Portsmouth Parish was the area west of what is currently Route 17, while St. Brides Parish is east of that line. Elizabeth River Parish is north of St. Brides Parish and contained the Borough (later city) of Norfolk. As with all areas, the border can and did change. These parishes each had a church associated with them and their own set of Overseers who all met periodically and assisted in taking care of the poor. Several Overseers were selected for each parish and if a person was selected and did not have a good reason for declining the appointment then he was fined. As expected all Overseers were men. You will also see instances in the accounts where an Overseer from one parish gave money to another parish, so these weren't regions competing with each other but operating for the good of Norfolk County.

In addition to overseers, you'll see other terms associated with caring for the poor. The sheriff and the collectors were the men in charge of collecting the tithe while the committee or board of the Overseers recommended the rate to be charged based on the number of "tithes" or "tythes" counted in the parish. In calculating the amount of the tithe, the overseers would estimate how many insolvents to expect based on their experience – the word meaning men who would be unable to pay the tithe they owed due to various reasons. Zachariah Douge for instance is listed in the book as needing assistance "having lost the use of his right arm and left leg and thigh due to the great cold while in the service of the United States." Since he was provided for by the Overseers of the Poor, he obviously was one of the poor who received assistance and would have been counted among the insolvents in the county. They also eliminated the men in certain jobs as directed by law, but the only one we saw listed was by Richard Webb who denoted that he had 6 constables who were exempt in 1798. One would also notice that the collectors received a commission on different things including collecting the tithe. It was not a "paid" job, but this was how the county compensated the men.

Code of Virginia Chapter 51 states that the year ends 31 March and the annual report should report the number provided for breaking out how many white and how many colored, for what length of time, where each was provided for or assisted, the name of each and the amount received for the year. These can be real goldmines for genealogists. A number of these reports reported the birth in the poor house of a child or the death of those involved. Some of these deaths were reported to the county (but not all) and are found in the Register of Deaths 1853-1860 and 1864-1870, such as that of John Glenard who was reported in the Parish House deaths as 10 Aug 1856. The death register for the county lists him as 27 years old but didn't list the cause of death. His death was reported by David Lynch who was listed as a "friend." Lynch was in fact the keeper of the Poor House in August 1857. Whether the Poor House records for that time are right (1856) or the death register (1857) was right is not known, but the death register does give more information. The births reported at the Poor House on the other hand do not seem to appear in the Register of Births 1853-1860 and 1864-1874 as we checked several of them.

The Poor House was supported by the county in the form of the tithables collected, but they also received money from the operation of the ferries as you will find "Ferry Money" received in some of the records. Money was also generated by the hire of the Parish Negroes which were hired out yearly with their names listed in the record or the rent of the Parish lands. You will also see the poor getting different amounts of money. This is most likely due to the circumstances or the number in the family. For example, one would get $56 for a year's support while another one would get $7. A lot of the people getting support from the parish were women with children or old or disabled citizens.

The poor were referred to by different terms, some listed as "an object" while others listed as widows, disabled, or children. When a child was no longer getting support from the Parish House, he or she might have been apprenticed out, died or taken in by relatives. All apprentice records for the county, like most county records do not survive. Also the Parish House could be called by different names – almshouse and "place of reception" are two which comes to mind. Some were supported at home by their family or friends and they were paid, such as Nathaniel Butt who was being kept by William Nichols. Butt was listed as both blind and lame.

Bookkeeping was not the best in the 1700s and 1800s. They often intermixed debits and credits although the books were set up to show debits (people getting money) on one side and credits (money coming in) on the other. We did not make any attempt to correct these, as we were not attempting to show how good or bad their bookkeeping or math was, only the important things from a genealogist's perspective. The dates things actually occurred were also sporadically recorded. As you know punctuation and spelling did not meet very high standards as these men were not selected for their writing or math skills so totals were eliminated in most cases in this book. Also punctuation was added when it helped to separate items or people.

Some surnames were "corrected" to be more in conformance with what we know of Norfolk County families. For example Western was corrected to Weston and Maning to Manning, but we did not change Ovelton to Overton as it was spelled consistently in the records as Ovelton and could have more to do with enunciation. Names such as Artzena Bailey were listed as spelled as we didn't know what her birth name was.... She was listed as Artzena, Arzen and later Zena depending on who was writing the names. Ferebee and Creekmur are consistently spelled the same in this book while Ginkins was most likely Jenkins, but we left it as written.

With the lack of punctuation there was doubt about what was meant. For example did items like "William Hare orphan" mean that William was an orphan or did it refer to the orphan of William Hare? When in doubt we listed it exactly as written in the record. A perfect example of the lack of punctuation causing issues is the following one dated 17 Jan 1803 – "Nathaniel Butt one of the overseers of the poor of Saint Brides Parish returned the following list of poor orphans to wit, Joshua Charles & Lovey Woodard, James Creekmur Ferebee, William Shadack, Tillet; Whereupon it is ordered that the Overseers of the poor of Saint Brides parish bind out the said orphans according to Law." In a day and age where middle names were rarely used (like punctuation) it is difficult to tell for sure how many orphans the Overseers wanted to bind out. Apprentice bonds between 1782 and 1818 are missing and we didn't find these orphans listed in the Minute Books, but we also can't be sure that the court agreed with binding them out or that the children survived long enough to be bound out. The first two are easy as we saw Joshua Charles and Lovey listed together in the Poor House, although he was always listed as Charles Woodard, but the other ones are puzzles. In 1797 and 1798 there was a James Creekmur, Sr. and a James Creekmur Jr. receiving assistance, but not a Ferebee. William Shadack could easily be Shadrack, but did not see either name in the Poor House records. And of course Tillet at the end is a puzzle. Tillet is a northeast NC name, but not a normal St. Brides Parish name. So how many orphans are there listed?

People went to the poor house when they lost their source of income, i.e. became a widow or an orphan, got sick with no one to care for them, etc. They left the poor house when they died, got better, found relatives to take them in, were apprenticed out, widow having given birth, etc. The babies left the same time the mother did. If several people came in together on the same date, especially if several were marked as small child, then they are most likely mother and child such as the Cox family Jane who attended the helpless with two small boys Wilson and Peter Cox.

You also see people in the poor house such as Ann Ancel along with what appears to be her children Lavinia and Alice with Alice being born in the poor house. They stay there a few years with the mother tending to the sick and then you see the mother later as Ann Ansell being assisted elsewhere. She was listed as being "at home" so she and her children went out on their own but were still needing assistance. Remember that spelling was not consistent, but phonetic which varied according to the person recording the info, but an educated guess says Ancel and Ansell are the same as they transitioned from one list to another. Ann evidently went into the poor house less than a month before her daughter was born.

You can also determine a time frame for a death of a person not getting assistance. For example, George Dyson turned in cash in St. Brides Parish in 1794 as well as authorizing payments in Portsmouth Parish in 1796. In early 1796, Dyson was still turning in cash to the Overseers, then on 7 Nov 1795, Col. W. Wilson turned in cash for Dyson and again on 2 Jan 1796, but on 15 Feb 1796 Capt. Hylton turned in cash for the "estate of etc." and Dyson disappears from the accounts. We added a footnote to that entry in the books explaining what likely happened to Dyson – again, it's reading between the lines and using multiple sources which is what genealogists do. Another example is "Mr. F. Hanbury (deceased)" in the office of the Overseer of the Poor in Pleasant Grove who a committee recommended replacing with Samuel J. Nichols at a meeting 21 May 1888." This is most likely Frederick who died 6 May 1888 at age 60 found in the death records for Norfolk County.

The rules of who they assisted and where (at home or at the Poor House) changed, so often you will find women with small children listed and since they only covered certain ages in caring for them at home, you will find the children listed by name along with their ages which is invaluable for tying people to their mothers.

As with all of our books, we'd like to thank the staff at the State Records Center of the Library of Virginia who pulled all these "unprocessed" records out for us and allowed us to photograph them in December of 2015. By allowing us to take images of these important files which could then sit on our computer untouched for almost 8 years until we got an interest (and time) in creating this book. We also would like to thank the research staff at the Library of Virginia who told us exactly what was available as we looked for vague terms like the poor.

One last bit of information .... In researching the poor of Norfolk County this year, we found that the Norfolk County Historical Society (NCHS) in Chesapeake also has poor house (alms house) records for the county for a later time period. As of this time, the society volunteers are arranging the records in protective sleeves and they plan to scan them in later and make them available. The time period which they have records available for do not duplicate or overlap the materials we got from the State Records Center for this book. Like all Norfolk County genealogists and historians, we appreciate the fact that they are taking the time and expense with volunteers to preserve these important records.

1786 Entries

At a meeting of the Overseers of the Poor for the Parish of St. Brides in the County of Norfolk at the house of Captain Joshua Grimes, Great Bridge on Thursday 13 July 1786, present: Charles Odeon, James Webb, Jr. Overseers.

The Overseers having examined and inquired into the situation of the poor house have allowed as follows:

Martha Bailey for the support of her two youngest children for this present year the sum of 50s

Daniel Cutherell for the keeping and maintaining Amy Cutherell who through old age and infirmities is not able to maintain herself, the sum of £8 for this present year.

Zachariah Douge who has lost the use of his right arm and left leg and thigh occasioned from great colds taken while in the service the United States, the sum of £10 for this present year.

Caleb Creekmur for the keeping and maintaining of William Cain, an orphan, in a low state of health, the sum of £5 for this present year.

Anne Smith who through old age and infirmities is not able to support herself, the sum of £6 for this present year.

Mary Fulford for the keeping and maintaining of Thomas Deale who through old age and infirmities is not able to support himself the sum of £5 for this present year.

We agree to a tax of 1s 3p on each tithable.

[signed] James Webb, Jr. & William Happer

1793 - 1794 Entries

[Pages are torn in half with the debits missing along with the name of the Parish][1]

	DEBITS	
	[Surviving debit side]	
	... from 1793-1794	£6.6
	... orphan children	£4.5/2
	... for John Dickens	£7.10
	... ing Sarah Taylor 1 year	£7.10
	... ments for keeping	£12
	... agreeable to an order of Court	£3
	... George Boush children	£1.16.5
	... Douge at different periods	£12
	... Pearce for keeping James .... child 3 mo.	£1.9.4
	... Widow McPherson for .... ldren	18s
	... granted Capt Hall for keeping.......Beesly from 3 Aug 93 to 3 Aug 94	£12
	...advanced George Etheridge an orphan	6s
	...attending a meeting of the Overseers	6s
	...attending a meeting of the Overseers	6s

[1] Based on the 1796 account this is the St. Brides Parish.

1794	CREDITS	
	Cash from Samuel Davis, treasurer	£24
	Cash from George Dyson	£30
	Cash from Capt. Hall	£12

Portsmouth Parish in account with George Wainwright

1793	DEBITS	
	Cash pd Elizabeth Ivey for Nancy Smith	£1
Sep	Cash pd James Smith for Nancy Smith	18s
Oct	Cash pd William Yates a balance in full for Mary Herd & child to 1 Sep 1793	£1.15
Nov	Cash pd James Smith for Nancy Smith	12s
Dec	Order in favor of George Townsend on said Davis	£1.16
1794		
Jun	Cash pd John Bowers as a balance in full for keeping Elizabeth Harris to the 1 Sep 1793	£14.18.9
	Cash pd John Elks for keeping William Wingate to Sep. 1793	£4
Jul	Cash pd John Deale as a balance for keeping Margaret Green to Sep 1793	£6.4
Aug	Cash pd John Deale as a balance for keeping Margaret Green to Sep 1794	£7.16
	Cash pd William Hodges as a balance in full for keeping William Farley to 1 Sep 1794	£17.2
	Cash pd John Bowers in full for keeping Elizabeth Harris to 1 Sep 1794	£6
	Cash pd John Bowers in full for William Wingate to 1 Sep 1794	£4
	Cash pd William Britton for John Bunting to 1 Sep	£12
	Cash pd James Smith in full for Nancy Smith to 1 Sep 1794	£12
	Cash pd George Townsend & Pernal Taylor for Wright Deans to 1 Sep 1794	£7.10
	Cash pd John Deale (an object) to 1 Sep 1794	£6
	Cash pd Joshua Taylor (an object) to 1 Sep 1794	£2.1.8
	Cash pd Hannah Price & 3 orphan children as a balance in full to 1 Sep 1794	£10.8
	Cash pd James Callahan for keeping Mourning Smith from 1 Jun 1793 to 1 Sep 1794	£3
	Cash pd William Yates in full for Margaret Herd and child to Sep 1794	£6
	Order in favor Robert Ives on George Dyson	£7.10
16 Feb	Sundries furnished Sarah McPherson	£1.3.9
19 Mar	Sundries furnished William Yeates for keeping Mary Herd up to this day	£3.19.1
30 Mar	Absolum Bruce for Smith Stafford	£2.4.3
Apr	Nancy Harris one of the poor	10s
11 Apr	John Spring one of the poor	£3.3.9

11 Apr	Paid Hannah Pierce one of the poor	£2.6
24 Apr	Cash pd Henry Consaul for a coffin for a poor child	3s
	Cash pd George Townsend for keeping Wright Deans for 1793	£2.11.9
1793	**CREDITS**	
Oct	Cash rec'd William Hoffler	£1.3.4
1794		
	Cash rec'd of Edmund Almond	£11.18.10½
Jun	Cash rec'd of Samuel Davis	£34.4.2
Aug	Cash rec'd of Samuel Davis	£91.8.8
	Order in favor of George Townsend on Samuel Davis	£1.16
	Order in favor of Robert Ives on George Dyson	£7.10

1794 - 1795 Entries

At a meeting of the Overseers of the Poor for Norfolk County held at Edmund Almond's 1 Sep 1794, present: Samuel Davis, William Langley, James Holt, Edmund Almond, George Ivy.

Ordered that the accounts of the Overseers of the Poor which has originated since the Court of Norfolk County agreed to furnish the Overseers with money for the use of poor, be recorded in this book for the inspection of said Court. The meeting finding no more business before them at present do adjourn until the 1st Monday in March next. *[signed]* Samuel Davis

At a meeting of the Overseers of the Poor for Norfolk County held at Edmund Almond's 2 Mar 1795, present: Samuel Davis, president, James Holt, Edmund Almond. There not being a sufficient number of members to make a meeting, adjourned until meeting agreeable to Act of Assembly. *[signed]* Samuel Davis

Portsmouth Parish in account with Samuel Davis

1794	**DEBITS**	
Sep	William Jones for keeping James Ward from December 1793	£8
1795		
	Dr. A. Slaughter for his attendance from Sep 1792 to Sep 1794	£16

Elizabeth River Parish in account with George Ivy

1794	**DEBITS**	
24 Jul	Cash pd Jinkins 3 children	£24
	Cash pd J. Spencer	£12
	John Grant's account	£9.18
	Attendance 7 days	£2.2
1795	**CREDITS**	
26 Jul	Cash from Samuel Davis, treasurer	£27
16 Sep	Cash from Samuel Davis, treasurer, by order of Sep Court	£21

Elizabeth River Parish in account with William *[torn]*

1794	**DEBITS**	
24 Jul	Cash pd Maximilian Marley's account	£22.10
	Cash pd Nathaniel Godfrey's account	£20.16.5/4
	Cash pd Mrs. Conley & son	£10
	Cash pd Miss Cooper's[2] 2 children	£5
	Cash pd Miss Millison	£3.15
	Cash pd Miss Kilgrow	£3
26 Jul	Cash pd John Cooper	£12
	Cash pd William Reid	18s
28 Jul	Cash pd Elizabeth Williams	£7.10
	Cash pd James Bartee for 1 lb corn for Mrs. Richardson	18s
12 Aug	Cash pd William Reid for 3 lbs corn	£2.14
	7 yards linen for Mrs. Millison for 2 shifts	10.6s
	Cash pd John Waddell on acct. Mrs. Brewer and Mrs. Riddle	£8.7.7
	Cash pd Mrs. Richardson	£1.12
	Cash pd Mrs. Brewer	£4.14.6
1 Sep	Cash pd Mary Conley	£5
	Cash pd for 7 yds linen, 1 pair shoes for Mrs. Climing & child	£1.1
	Cash pd burying Mrs. Millson	£1.15
	Cash pd Mrs. Cooper's & 2 children	£2.10
	Cash pd Mrs. Richardson	£1.5
	10 days attendance	£3.0
18 Oct	Cash pd Mrs. Conley	12s
29 Oct	Cash pd Lovey Brewer for nursing mother	12s
3 Nov	Cash pd Mary Conley	£1.10
28 Nov	Cash pd Mary Conley	£1.10
23 Dec	Cash pd Mary Conley	£1.8.6
1795		
7 Jan	Cash pd Mrs. Kilgrow for John Kilgrow	£1.4
	Cash pd Mrs. Richardson	£1.4
	Cash pd Mrs. Conley	6s
13 Feb	Cash pd James Guy 1 pr shoes	6s
	Cash pd Mrs. Cooper for 2 children	£2.8
	Cash pd Mrs. Conley	£3 4/2
	Cash pd Mrs. Conley house rent	£1.10

Portsmouth Parish in account with Samuel Davis

1794	**DEBITS**	
10 Oct	Cash pd Jinkins Maria[3] for to remove out of the county	11s
	Cash pd Anthony Millow for people to set up with him	4s

[2] There are several instances in these records where a woman is listed as Miss with children and later listed as Mrs. Of course it could be just people with the same name, but it does appear unusual.

[3] This one appears to have first and last names reversed, but it's what was in the record.

	Cash pd Anthony Millow for digging his grave	3s
20 Nov	Order on Willis Wilson for said Millow	£1.4
	Order on Geo. Dyson for R. Borland making coffin for Millow	12s 6p
21 Nov	Cash pd Mary Combs 1 month	12s
	Cash pd Joseph Carter one of the poor	£2.2
	Cash pd Joseph Britton 1 month	12s
	Cash pd Mary Moore for James Etherington's orphans for keeping 3 months	£1.10
13 Dec	Cash pd for Sampson Culpepper	£1.16
24 Dec	Cash pd Mary Combs 1 month	12s
	Cash pd Joseph Britton 1 month	12s
29 Dec	Cash pd Willis Wilson for Ann Millow for the support of her 2 children	£1.4
	Cash pd George Dyson for William Jones for keeping James Ward until 25 Dec	£4
1795		
23 Jan	Cash pd Mary Combs 1 month	12s
	Cash pd Joseph Britton 1 month	12s
29 Jan	Cash pd Willis Wilson for Joseph Carter	£1.4
18 Feb	Cash pd George Dyson for Mary Moore for James Etherington	£1.10
23 Feb	Cash pd James Weston to remove him	18s
24 Feb	Cash pd Mary Combs 1 month	12s
28 Feb	Cash pd Joseph Britton 1 month	12s
7 Mar	Cash pd Willis Wilson for Joseph Carter & family	£1.4
	Cash pd for a book	9s
	Cash pd for Clerk	£2.8

1795 - 1796 Entries

Portsmouth Parish in account with Thomas Cherry

1792[4]	**DEBITS**	
14 Jul	Cash pd Mrs. Manning for Ann Isdel	13s 6p
1794		
24 May	Cash pd Lawrence Fowler	12s
	Cash pd Corbin Bracket for board etc for Peter Leavous *[?]*	£1.4.6
12 Jun	Cash pd William Peck for nursing Selah Payro	£1.2
	Cash pd coffin and digging grave	14s 6p
24 Jun	Cash pd James Brown for keeping Joseph Carter	18s
27 Jun	Cash pd Mrs. Manning Dr. Herbert & Winget	£27.19.6
2 Aug	Cash pd to board of Joseph Carter 4 weeks	£1.4
	Shirt for Joseph Carter	7s 6p
8 Sep	Board Hannah W. David 10 days, a sick woman	£1.5
18 Sep	Carrying her to Mrs. Manning's & back	6s

[4] This is either a mistake on the year or a very misplaced entry.

	Carrying her to William Creekmur's	3s
10 Oct	Sundries expensed attending on her place	£4.8
11 Oct	Sundries expensed on Ginkins Marca on her place	£1.3.3
	5 lbs beef for Joshua Brown	13½p
28 Dec	Cash pd Solomon Whaley for keeping Eliza Staples 2 months	£3
	An order on George Dyson for Joshua Brown	£3
1795		
4 Feb	Cash pd James Brown for keeping Joseph Carter	£2.5
17 Feb	An order on George Dyson for Mary Richardson	£3
18 Feb	Cash pd Cloe Dale	6s
	Order on George Dyson for Cloe Dale	£2.5
	Cash that will become due the last day of Mar for keeping Eliza Staples	£1.4
1796		
26 Jun	Cash rec'd from Samuel Davis	£33.1.6
Nov	Sundry orders on Mr. George Dyson	£8.5
28 Dec	Cash rec'd from Mr. Dyson	£15
7 Mar	Cash pd Thomas Cherry for the benefit of Elizabeth Staples	£6.11.4½

Portsmouth Parish in account with James S. Mathews

1795	**DEBITS**	
	Cash pd Elizabeth Cassel & 3 children for their maintenance 4 months viz from Jul 21 to Nov 21	£3.12
	Cash pd Elizabeth Cassel 1 month	9s
	Cash pd Joseph Carter per order of Court 5 months from 1 Aug 1795 to 1 Apr 1796	£7.10
	Cash pd Joseph Carter up to 1 Apr 1796 3 months	£2.5
	Cash pd Keziah Reed from 1 Aug 1795 to 1 Apr 1796	£7.4
	Cash pd Elizabeth House & 3 children from 20 Jul 1795 to 20 Mar 1796	£7.4
	Cash pd Ann Millow & 2 children from 7 Aug 1795 to 7 Jan 1796	£3
	Cash pd Elizabeth Wilkins, a disabled woman, from 8 Aug 1795 to 8 Mar 1796	£3.3
	Cash pd Elizabeth Duffle a sick woman	£1.4
	Cash pd for winding sheet to bury her	6s 9p
	Cash pd Elizabeth Moore for keeping James Arlington, orphan, from 21 May 1795 to 21 Nov 1795	£3
	Cash pd Mary Combs & Joseph Britton (man & wife) as per order of Court from 1 Sep 1795 to 1 Mar 1796	£7.4
	Cash pd Mary Combs from 1 Mar 1796 to 1 May 1796	£1.4
	Cash pd N. Wood digging 4 graves viz: E. Duffle's, C. Denney's, Mrs. Lynch, Mrs. Cassel's child	12s
	Cash pd Wilson Williams making 4 coffins viz: C. Denney's, Sally Richardson, Mrs. Cassel's 2 children	£2.2

	Cash pd John C. Bustin for a coffin for Linch's child	7s 6p
	Cash pd Wakefield to buy necessaries for C. Denney when sick	3s
	Cash pd Fatherly for giving Overseers notice of a meeting 29 Sep 1795	9s
	Cash pd Zebro Kellum from 1 Oct 1795 to 1 Apr 1796	£2.14
	Cash pd William Jones per George Dyson for keeping James Ward from 25 Dec 1794 to 25 Sep 1795	£6
	Cash pd Mathew Howard, a blind man, from 2 Oct 1795 to 2 Apr 1796	£3.12
	Cash pd Elizabeth Wood for James Wood, a sick man, from 17 Nov 1795 to 7 Jan 1796	£1.16
	Cash pd Ann Wakefield for keeping William Hare, orphan, from 20 Nov 1795 to 7 Jan 1796	£1
	Cash pd Wakefield for keeping William Hare from 1 Jan to 1 Mar 1796	£1.4
	Cash pd Dr. Leigh a quarter salary	£2.2
	Cash pd Mary Shays for keeping Elizabeth Shays' orphan up to 20 Dec 5 months	£1.10
	Cash pd Mrs. Peed for keeping Mr. Reid, a poor sick man, 13 weeks	£3
	Cash pd Louisa Archy & 2 children for 1 month to 12 Feb 1796	12s
	Cash pd Nancy Wright, a poor woman	6s
	Cash pd Ann Millow, a poor sick woman with a child, from 7 Jan 1796 to 7 Apr 1796	18s
	Cash pd Elizabeth House 1 month	18s
	7 days attendance	£2.2

Portsmouth Parish in account with James S. Mathews

1796	**DEBITS**	
	Cash pd William Watts for Ann Millow, a poor sick woman, from 7 Apr to 7 May	£1.4
	Cash pd Joseph Carter for 6 months from 1 Apr to 1 Oct	£5.5
	Cash pd Deborah Kellum for 6 months 1 Apr to 1 Oct	£2.14
	Cash pd Mathew Howard for 7 months from 2 Apr to 2 Nov	£4.4
	Cash pd Keziah Reed for 7 months from 6 Apr to 6 Nov	£6.6
	Cash pd Elizabeth Wilkins for 5 months from 8 Apr to 8 Sep	£2.5
	Cash pd Louisa Archy for 7 months from 23 Feb to 25 Sep	£4.4
	Cash pd Thomas Cherry 6 months from 21 Apr to 21 Oct	£3.12
	Cash pd Elizabeth House 6 months from 10 Apr to 20 Oct	£9
25 Apr	Cash pd Andrew Kidd, clerk, for stationary, etc	7s 9p
22 Jul	Cash pd Col. J. Butt, Overseer of the Poor	£22.10
	Cash pd Mary Combs 6 months from 2 May to 2 Nov	£5.8.

	Cash pd for Nelson Thornton, orphan, 5 months from 13 May to 13 Oct	£4.4
	Cash pd for John Harnage & 2 children from 13 May to 13 Oct	£5.8
	Cash pd for James Reed (7 May)	12s
	Cash pd to and for Joshua Thornton from 9 Jun to 4 Sep and for his funeral expenses	£8.4.6
	Cash pd Thomas Wakefield for William Hare, orphan, from 1 Mar to 1 Jul	£2.8
	Cash pd for Nancy Thornton, board, coffin and funeral expenses	£1.11
1795	**CREDITS**	
	Cash rec'd of George Dyson	£4.10
	Cash rec'd of Col. W. Wilson	£4.10
1 Sep	Cash rec'd of George Dyson	£3
	Cash rec'd of Col. W. Wilson	£3
22 Sep	Cash rec'd of George Dyson	£6
	Cash rec'd of Jonathan Rogers for the sale of Mrs. Lynch's furniture	£1
3 Oct	Cash rec'd of Col. W. Wilson	£6
	Order on George Dyson in favor William Jones for keeping James Ward	£6
24 Nov	Cash rec'd of Col. W. Wilson	£9
23 Jan	Cash rec'd of George Dyson	£16
1 Mar	Cash rec'd of Col. W. Wilson	£9
	Cash rec'd of George Dyson	£9
31 Mar	Cash rec'd of Col. W. Wilson	£15
9 May	Cash rec'd of Col. W. Wilson	£15
28 Jun	Cash rec'd of Col. W. Wilson	£45
21 Sep	Cash rec'd of Col. W. Wilson	£30

Elizabeth River Parish in account with Edward Valentine

1796	**DEBITS**	
12 Mar	Cash, etc. furnished James Guy from 26 Sep up to this day	£4.2.½
	Cash furnished Samuel Jones for his support from 12 Oct 1795 up to this day	£3.7.6.
	Cash pd Mary Clemonds from 12 Oct 1795 up to this date at different times for the support of John Jones, a poor child	£3
	Cash furnished Mary Clemonds from 12 Oct 1795, up to the 12th of the present month	£3.7.6
	Cash advanced to Lovey Brewer for her support from 23 Dec 1795 to 23 Feb 1796	£1.17.6
	Cash advanced to Mrs. Ridley per J. Jones	13s 6p
	Cash pd Mrs. Pool in part for board and nursing John Kilgrow when under the smallpox	£1.12

	Cash pd Elijah Bennet for the inoculation and attendance on 2 Negro children	£2.16
	Cash pd Willet & O'Connor for advertising the Parish Negroes to hire, land to rent and blank bonds	10s 6p
	Cash pd George Wilson for coffin for L. Duncan	12s
	Cash Thomas Butt for coffin for Churmuck	12s
	Attendance at the meeting of the Overseers of the Poor	£2.2
1795	**CREDITS**	
31 Oct	Cash rec'd this day of Col. Wilson	*[torn]*
1796		
Mar	James Douglas' bond	*[torn]*

St. Brides Parish in account with Josiah Butt

1796	**DEBITS**	
12 Mar	Cash pd James Sykes from 14 Jul to 12 Feb sundry payments	£7.19
	Cash pd Frances Boush	£4.5.9
	Cash pd Sarah McPherson from 8 Jul to 25 Nov	£5.1
	Cash pd John Dickens from 16 Jul to 25 Feb 1796	£10.0.1½
	Cash pd Zachariah Douge from 30 Nov 1795 to 17 Feb 1796	£7.4
	Cash pd Thomas Freeman including doctor's bill, nurse's bill, and tailor's bill including also a coffin for him.	£10.13.3
	Cash pd Timothy Wood for keeping David & John Dennis, 2 orphans, from 16 Dec to 5 Mar 1796	£6.5
30 Mar	Cash pd Rachel Burgess	£1.4
12 Feb	Cash pd Willis Sykes at sundry payments	£2.16.8½
	Cash pd Willis Sykes coffin & digging his grave	15s
	Cash pd Abiah Creekmur from 12 Sep to 30 Jan 1796, at sundry payments	£5.6.6
2 Feb	Cash pd Mary Creekmur	£1
	Cash pd Abiah Timberlake from 2 Sep 1795 to 12 Feb 1796	£4.18.6
12 Feb	Cash pd Mathew Creekmur	12s
	Cash pd John Smith for keeping Sarah Rose	£3.14.6
	Cash pd John Smith for a coffin & digging grave for Sarah Rose	18s
	Cash pd Herbert Tooley for keeping George Etheridge 26 days	£2.12
	Cash pd Herbert Tooley for coffin, winding sheet and digging grave for George Etheridge	£1.7
	Cash pd Dr. Dessenis' bill for medicine and attendance on poor of St. Brides Parish	£9

1795	**CREDITS**	
Jul	Cash rec'd of George Dyson for the use of the poor of St. Brides Parish	£15
	Cash rec'd of Col. W. Wilson	£14.14.2
24 Nov	Cash rec'd of Col. W. Wilson	£15
25 Nov	Cash rec'd of George Dyson	£15
1796		
15 Feb	Cash rec'd of Col. W. Wilson	£15

St. Brides Parish in account with James Grimes, Sr.

1795	**DEBITS**	
	Cash pd Levy Etheridge for 3 months	£3.6
	Cash pd William Etheridge from 1 Dec to 1 Mar 1796	£2.8
1796		
	6 days attendance	£1.16
20 Apr	Cash pd Henry Creekmur for 10½ months	£12.12
29 May	Cash pd Mary Hodges for 9 months	£3.15
21 Jun	Cash pd Henry McPherson (now dead)	£3.13
	Cash pd doctor's bill for Elizabeth McPherson	£12.19.6
	Cash pd William Etheridge, orphan, for his board 1 year	£12
	Cash pd transporting Elizabeth McPherson 16 miles and returning	15s
7 Mar	3 days attendance	18s
	CREDITS	
7 Mar	Cash rec'd of John Shield	£16.13.1½

St. Brides Parish with Thomas Bartee (Overseer)

1796	**DEBITS**	
21 Mar	7 days attendance	£2.2
	Cash to Kesiah Cutril for Ed Whitehurst	19s 9p
	Cash to Kesiah Cutril for Ed Whitehurst	10s 3p
	CREDITS	
	Cash rec'd of John Shield	£1.10

Portsmouth Parish in account with John Shield

1795	**DEBITS**	
30 Apr	Cash pd Stephen Anderson	12s
7 May	Cash pd William Plummer for E. Staples	£1.10
20 May	Cash pd Stephen Anderson	12s
26 May	Cash pd Cloe Deale	12s
1 Jun	Cash pd Joshua Brown	18s
15 Jun	Cash pd Elizabeth Moore for Hetherington's orphans	£1.2.6
	Cash pd Elizabeth House	£1.4
19 Jun	Cash pd Stephen Anderson	£1.10
	Cash pd Elizabeth Moore for Hetherington's orphans	6s
27 Jun	Cash pd Elizabeth Cassel & 3 children	18s

	Cash pd Elizabeth Wilkins	6s 3p
29 Jun	Cash pd Joseph Carter, wife & children	£1.15.6
30 Jun	Cash pd Cloe Deale	£1
2 Jul	Cash pd Mary Combs	£1.4
	Cash pd Joseph Britton	£1.4
9 Jul	Cash pd Joshua Brown	12s 7p
11 Jul	Cash pd Ann Millow & 2 children	12s
23 Jul	Cash pd William Plummer for E. Staples	£2.9.2
27 Jul	Cash pd Stephen Anderson	12s
4 Aug	Cash pd Cloe Deale & 2 children	15s
6 Aug	Cash pd William Deale	£1.4
14 Aug	Cash pd Stephen Anderson	6s
27 Aug	Cash pd William Trigler	6s
31 Aug	Cash pd Stephen Anderson	6s
	Cash pd Cloe Deale	6s
2 Sep	Cash pd William Trigler	18s
3 Sep	Cash pd William Deale	6s
17 Sep	Cash pd William Trigler	£1.4
25 Sep	Cash pd Joshua Brown & wife	18s
12 Oct	Cash pd William Trigler	6s
7 Nov	Cash pd Joseph Carter 1 shirt	6s
	Cash pd Joseph Carter 1 jacket	14s
	Cash pd Joseph Carter 1 trousers & shoes	19s 6p
11 Nov	Cash pd Mrs. Wood	12s
20 Nov	Cash pd Mrs. Brown	6s
28 Nov	Cash pd Dr. Leigh	£2.2
	Cash pd Mrs. Cutril	£1
18 Dec	Cash pd Stephen Anderson	18s
22 Dec	Cash pd Mary Ward	18s
1796		
1 Jan	Cash pd William Plummer for Joseph Carter, Sr.	£2.8
2 Jan	Cash pd Mrs. Cutril for keeping Upton's child	£1.10
	Cash pd carrying Peggy Baker out of this state	£3.12
22 Jan	Cash pd Stephen Anderson	£1
24 Jan	Cash pd Mary Ward	£1.6
	Cash pd Margaret Cadenhead	1.10
4 Feb	Cash pd Mary Brown	9s 9p
24 Feb	Cash pd Stephen Anderson	18s
27 Feb	Cash pd William Plummer for Joseph Carter Sr.	£2.2
4 Mar	Cash pd Mary Ward	£1.4
10 Mar	Cash pd Elizabeth Brown for keeping an orphan	15s
15 Mar	Cash pd John Deale for the former Overseers	£1.10
21 Mar	7 days attendance	£2.2
	Order on George Dyson for Joseph Carter & wife	£1.10
	Order on Mary Combs	£1.4
	Order on Joseph Britton	£1.4
	Order on Mary Combs	£1.4
	Order on Joseph Britton	£1.4

	Order on Joseph Carter wife etc.	£1.10
	Order on Willis Wilson for Stephen Anderson	£1.4
	Order in favor of Solomon Whaley for Elizabeth Staples	£4.18.6
	Order on George Dyson in favor of Joseph Upton	£1.4
	CREDITS	
15 Jun	Cash rec'd Mr. George Dyson	£10.4.3
29 Aug	Cash rec'd Mr. George Dyson	£3
7 Nov	Cash rec'd of Col. W. Wilson for G. Dyson	£9
1796		
2 Jan	Cash rec'd of Col. W. Wilson for Mr. George Dyson	£9
15 Feb	Cash rec'd of Captain Hylton for estate of etc.[5]	£9
	Amount sundry orders on George Dyson	£9
28 Apr	Cash rec'd of Col. W. Wilson	£6
2 Jul	Cash rec'd of Col. W. Wilson	£6
10 Sep	Cash rec'd of Col. W. Wilson	£3
	Amount orders drawn on W. Wilson	£6.2.6

Elizabeth River Parish in Account with John Wilkins [Overseer]

1795	**DEBITS**	
1 Jun	Cash pd to Mrs. Colney *[sic]* & daughter at sundry times from 1 Jun 1795 to 1 Jul 1796	£21.13.4
10 Oct	Cash pd Samuel Wilder & 2 sons from 10 Oct 1795 until 1 Jun 1796 in full to this date	£11.12.6
1796		
27 Jan	Cash pd Mrs. Cooper for keeping her two children from 1 Apr 1795 to 1 Jan 1796	£5.8
28 Jan	Cash pd John Colney by Mr. Wilbins *[sic]* order for boarding John Kilgrow, orphan, 6 months to 1 Jan 1796 in full	£3
7 Mar	Cash pd Elizabeth Williams for 6 months boarding Edward Dewier in full to the 1 Jan 1796	£2.8
10 Mar	Cash pd Elizabeth Drayton, a poor object	6s
10 Jun	Cash pd Mrs. Churnick from 1 Apr 1796 to 1 Jul 1796 In full	£2.14
12 Jun	Cash pd James Cooper for boarding Dinah Cooper & John Cooper from 1 Jan 1796 to 1 Jul 1796	£18
20 Jun	Cash pd Joshua Peter for 1 month in full to 1 Jul 1796	12s
1 Jul	Cash pd Mrs. Colney & daughter for July	£1.13.4

[5] This is most likely from the estate of George Dyson. It appears that Dyson was paying the funds he had collected for the poor through 29 Aug 1795. On 7 Nov (95) and again on 2 Jan (96) the money Dyson had collected for the poor was paid by Col. Wilson. On 19 Apr 1796, an administrator bond was issued to Augustine Slaughter indicating that the intestate Dyson had died (Sharon Gable and Truitt Bonney, *Norfolk County Virginia (extant) Administrator Bonds 1711-1850* (Suffolk, Virginia: privately published, 2008), p 48.).

	1 day attendance at the annual meeting at Mr. Mushrow's & ferriage	6s 9p
	1 day attendance at the Borough Tavern hiring out the Parish Negroes	6s
	Taking bonds for the Parish Negroes	6s
	1 day attendance at the meeting at Mr. Mushrow's & ferriage	6s 9p
	1 days attendance at the meeting at Mr. Mushrow's & ferriage	6s 9p
	Horse hire & ferriage on the parish business	3s 9p
1795	**CREDITS**	
3 Nov	Cash rec'd of Col. W. Wilson	£15
1796		
5 Jan	Cash rec'd of Mr. Mitchel for hire Negro Lewis, a Parish Negro	£7.10
6 Jan	Cash rec'd of Mrs. Cone for the rent of a house, the property of John Kilgrow, orphan	£1
27 Feb	Cash rec'd of Dr. Taylor for hire Negro Gasper one of the Parish Negroes	£15.15
9 Apr	Cash rec'd of Mr. Ritson for hire of the one the Parish Negroes	£7
1 Jun	Cash rec'd of James Woodward for hire of Negro Davie for 1795	£22

Elizabeth River Parish in account with Edward Valentine, Overseer

1796	**DEBITS**	
	Cash advanced James Guy at different times from 11 Mar to 12 Sep	£4.14.6
	Cash advanced Samuel Jones at different times from 12 Mar to 12 Aug	£4.1
	Cash advanced Mrs. Clemonds at different times from 12 Mar to 12 Sep, allowance to J. Jones	£5.2
	Cash advanced Mrs. Clemonds at different times from 12 Mar to 12 Sep (for her)	£5.3.7½
	Cash advanced S. Jones & William Godfrey different times from 12 Mar to 12 Sep, 8 months allowance to Mrs. Ridley	£5.8
	Cash advanced to Lovey Brewer different times from 24 Mar to 24 Jul, for 4 months allowance, nursing & burying charges included	£6.7.6
	Cash advanced to Mrs. Churnick's thru 2 Apr last, she belonging to Mr. Wilkins' list	12s
	Cash advanced to James Davis for keeping Henry Davis, a poor child, from 10 Feb 1795 to 10 Feb 1796	£10
	Cash pd for the revised laws	£2.8
	Cash pd F. Reynolds for a coffin for Patty Robinson	12s
	Cash pd Haycock for helping to bury Patty Robinson	3s

	The above named Patty Robinson was a poor person belonging to Princess Anne County who died in the Parish aforesaid. The said county of Princess Anne being by law bound to refund to E.R. Parish the above 15s.	
	Cash pd F. Reynolds for making 2 coffins one for Lovey Brewer the other for S. Jones	£1.4

Portsmouth Parish in account with John Shield, Overseer

1796	**DEBITS**	
31 Mar	Cash pd Mrs. Cutril for keeping an orphan	£1.10
7 Apr	Cash pd Mary Ward per order	18s
	2½ yards Oznaburghs to John Carter, Sr.	2s 6p
18 May	Cash pd Mary Ward per order	18s
28 Jun	Cash pd Mrs. Cutril for keeping orphan	£2.2
28 Jun	Cash pd printer for advertising notice, etc.	6s
1 Jul	Cash pd Mary Ward	18s
2 Jul	Cash pd John Deale	£3.18
6 Jul	Cash pd Thomas Bartee	£1.10
9 Jul	Cash pd John Talbot, an Overseer	£15
27 Jul	Cash pd Andrew Kidd, clerk, as part of his salary	19s 10p
29 Jul	Cash pd William Plummer for John Carter, Sr.	£1.19.7½
30 Jul	Cash pd Mary Balentine	13s 3p
5 Aug	Cash pd Mary Ward	18s
10 Aug	Cash pd Elizabeth Wilder	13s 3p
31 Aug	Cash pd Jo. Cassel	6s
3 Sep	Cash pd Mary Carter	6s
9 Sep	Cash pd Joseph Cassel	12s
21 Sep	Cash pd Mrs. Cutril for orphan	£1.4
	Cash pd Col. J. Butt for G. Marchant	£30
22 Sep	Cash pd Thomas Cherry old account	18s 10p
23 Sep	Cash pd John Talbot for his poor	£30
3 Oct	Cash pd John Taylor for E. Rose	£3
	Cash pd Edward Valentine	£3
	Cash pd John Wilkins	£3
	Cash pd Benjamin Crow for a coffin for Sally Wilder	12s
7 Oct	Cash pd Dr. Leigh, the balance of his years' salary	£3.16
15 Oct	Cash pd Mary Ward	£1.10
7 Apr	Order of Col. Wilson in favor of Mary Ward	18s
18 May	Order of Col. Wilson in favor of Mary Ward	18s
	CREDITS	
28 Jun	Cash rec'd of Col. W. Wilson	£30
21 Sep	Cash rec'd of Col. W. Wilson	£97.10

St. Brides Parish in account with Josiah Butt Overseer

1796	DEBITS	
	Cash pd James Sykes at sundry times from 26 Mar to 30 Sep	£10.13
	Cash pd Frances Boush at sundry times from 26 Mar to 20 Sep	£10
	Cash pd John Dickens at sundry times from 29 Apr to 30 Sep	£8.17
	Cash pd Abiah Creekmur at sundry times from 25 Apr to 26 Jul	£4.6.6
	Cash pd Ann Timberlake at sundry times from 29 Mar to 23 Sep	£5.2.6
10 May	Cash pd Mathew Creekmur at sundry payments	£6.6
	Cash pd Zachariah Douge at sundry payments from 5 Jul to 2 Sep	£6.16
	Cash pd David & John Dennis from 17 May to 15 Jul	£5.18
	Cash pd for John Baxter viz shirt, making his coffin and digging grave	£1.4.6
15 May	Cash pd coffin and digging grave for Fanny Suggs	£1.2.6
16 Sep	Cash pd Joseph Hodges	£1.10
	CREDITS	
21 Apr	Cash rec'd Col. W. Wilson	£13.4
2 Jul	Cash rec'd Mr. James Mathews, Overseer of Poor	£22.10
Sep	Cash rec'd Mr. John Shield, Overseer of Poor	£30

Portsmouth Parish in account with John Talbot

1795	DEBITS	
21 May	Order on George Dyson in favor Robert Berland for making coffin for Mr. Dowdall	12s
23 May	Order on George Dyson in favor Robert Berland for funeral charges	3s 9p
24 May	Cash pd John Spring at sundry times	£6.12.6
2 Jun	Cash pd Ann Harris at sundry times	£8.14.6
23 Jun	Cash pd Joseph Thompson for Milly Hazelgrove 3 weeks board	£1.4
24 Jun	Cash pd George Joliffe for keeping Rhody Mackie	£3.12
	Cash pd Hannah Pierce & 3 children	£9.5.9
26 Jun	Cash pd Hannah Culpeper (now dead)	£2.7.10
	Cash pd Sarah Welch sundry times	£7.4.7½
29 Jun	Cash pd Mary Millow	£4.5.6
	Cash pd Ann Wakefield for William Hare's orphan	8s
3 Jul	Cash pd Samuel Stafford for keeping Smith Stafford	£4.13
20 Sep	Cash pd George Townsend for keeping Wright Deans	£8.14.3½
1796		
19 Jan	Cash pd Mary Bowers for keeping Sarah Ivey	£3
25 Jan	Cash pd Mary Callahan for Elizabeth Griffin including coffin & funeral charges	£1.10.8

25 Feb	Cash pd John Deale for keeping Margaret Deale, orphan[6]	11s 3p
	Cash pd Mary Bental and 3 children	£2.4
1796		
	Cash pd Sarah Welch in full to 1 Apr 1796	£2.15.5½
	Cash pd George Townsend for keeping Wright Deans	5s 3p
29 Feb	Cash pd Samuel Stafford for keeping Smith Stafford	£4.16
30 Mar	Cash pd John Spring	£1.4
	Cash pd Elizabeth Rose, poor woman	6s
	Cash pd Hannah Pierce in full to 1 Apr	15s
1 Apr	Cash pd Ann Harris in full to 1 Apr	£1.5.6
	Cash pd John Deale for keeping Margaret Deale	12s
17 Apr	Cash pd Mary Bental and 3 children	12s
18 May	Cash pd George Townsend in full for Wright Deans to 1 Apr	£3.5.8
14 May	Cash pd Hannah Pierce in part for 1796	£1.13.3
16 May	Cash pd Mary Bental	£1.10
29 May	Cash pd Sarah Welch in part for 1796	£1.5.6
31 May	Cash pd George Townsend for Wright Deans for 1796	£3.5.8
23 Jun	Cash pd Elisha Smith, a poor man,	£1.5.6
	Cash pd John Spring in full to 1 Apr	£1.3.6
	Cash pd Mary Bowers in full for keeping Sarah Ivey to 1 Apr	£6
24 Jul	Cash pd Elizabeth Stafford in full for Smith Stafford to 1 Apr 1796	£2.11
	Cash pd Samuel Bufkin for keeping Milly Hazelgrove	£2.2
25 Jul	Cash pd George Joliffe for keeping Rhody Mackie to 1 Apr 1796	£2.2
	Cash pd Henry Pulling in full for keeping Lavina Ross to 1 Apr 1796	£1.7.6
	Cash pd Robert Hargroves for moving Margaret Tucker from Nansemond County to this county[7]	6s
24 Sep	Cash pd Hannah Pierce in part for 1796	£3.0.9
27 Sep	Cash pd Nathan Rose in part for Elizabeth Rose	£2.2
	Cash pd Sarah Welch in part for 1796	£1.10
	Cash pd George Townsend for Wright Deans 1796	£2.5.3
	Cash pd Mary Bental	£1.10
	Cash pd Ann Isdel in part for 1796	£1.16
	Cash pd John Spring in part for 1796	8s
12 Oct	Cash pd Elizabeth Stafford for Smith Stafford in part	£2.13
16 Oct	Cash pd William Britton for keeping John Bunting	£5.16
27 Oct	Cash pd Mary Callahan sundry times	£2.0.4½

[6] Often when a person of one surname is being paid to keep a person of the same surname, you can find a relationship.

[7] The counties were required to take back the poor who moved to another county but had not set up the required residency. You will see several examples in this book.

14 Nov	Cash pd John Jones for Elizabeth Ivey in full to 5 Mar 1796	£5
3 Dec	Cash pd Margaret Tucker for keeping Samuel Creekmur as per account	£2
	Cash pd Edward Moore for keeping Sarah Ives, orphan, in full to 5 Mar 1796	£7
	Cash pd John Bowers for keeping William Wingate in full to 1 Apr 1796	£2.18.4
13 Dec	Cash pd Elizabeth Stafford for keeping Smith Stafford in part for 1796	12s
28 Dec	Cash pd George Townsend for Wright Deans in part	£2.2
30 Dec	Cash pd John Spring in part for 1796	£1.4
1797		
5 Jan	Cash pd William Britton for keeping John Bunting	£2.8
6 Jan	Cash pd Hannah Pierce in part for 1796	£1.4
12 Jan	Cash pd Elizabeth Stafford for Smith Stafford	£1.1
14 Jan	Cash pd John Deale in part his account	£3.2
19 Jan	Cash pd Nathan Rose in part for Mary Bental	£1.16
	Cash pd John Graham for Ann Harris	£1.4
	Cash pd Mary Callahan in full for Thomas Griffin, orphan, to 1 Jan 1797	£2.19.7½
	Cash pd John Deale in part (omitted 4 Jun 1796)	£1.14
	Cash pd George Townsend a balance in full due from George Wainwright late overseer	£4.4
	5 days attendance	£1.10
1795	**CREDITS**	
21 May	Order on George Dyson in favor of Robert Borland for coffin for Mrs. Dowdal	12s
	Order on George Dyson in favor of Robert Borland for funeral for Mrs. Dowdal	3s 9p
	Cash rec'd from George Dyson	£9
15 Jun	Cash rec'd from George Dyson	£9
13 Aug	Cash rec'd from George Dyson	£4.10
	Cash rec'd from Willis Wilson	£4.10
21 Nov	Cash rec'd from George Dyson	£9
21 Dec	Cash rec'd from George Dyson	£9
1796		
18 Jan	Cash rec'd from George Dyson	£11
26 Mar	Cash rec'd from Willis Wilson	£21
14 May	Cash rec'd from Willis Wilson	£25.4
9 Jul	Cash rec'd from John Shield	£15
	Cash rec'd from John Shield	£30
	Cash rec'd from John Shield	£21

1796-1797 Entries

Portsmouth Parish in account with John Shield

1796	DEBITS	
22 Oct	Cash pd John Grant Dr. Taylor's bond per order Lemuel Denby	£20.10
	Cash pd William Plummer for keeping Joseph Carter, Sr. in full	£4.0.3¾
	Cash pd for linen for John Carter	13s 11½p
5 Nov	Cash pd Joseph Cassel	£1.16
20 Nov	Cash pd for leather for Joseph Cassel	3s 6p
5 Dec	Cash pd Joseph Cassel (since dead)	18s
14 Dec	Cash pd Mary Ward	18s
17 Dec	Cash pd Mary Cattenhead	£2.2
	Cash pd Andrew Kidd in full for one year salary as clerk to the Overseers of the Poor	£5.0.2
22 Dec	Cash pd Stephen Anderson	18s
27 Dec	Cash pd James Mathews for his poor	£15
	Cash pd John Talbot for his poor	£21
1797		
6 Jan	Cash pd James Taylor for E. Rose	£3.5
12 Jan	Cash pd James Brown for Peggy Brown	£1.16
12 Jan	Cash pd John Millow for keeping Esther Brown	£3
13 Jan	Cash pd William Willey	12s
24 Jan	Cash pd Mary Ward	18s
25 Jan	Cash pd Stephen Anderson	£1.4
1 Feb	Cash pd Mary Brown for orphan	7s 6p
4 Feb	Cash pd James S. Mathews 2 bonds	£11.18
22 Feb	Cash pd Stephen Anderson	18s
23 Feb	Cash pd Margaret Cassel	10s 6p
	Cash pd Anna Bartee	£2.2
	Cash pd James Grimes, Overseer of the Poor	£16.13.1½
	Cash pd James Boushell	£1.13
	Cash pd John Talbot	£7.10
	Cash pd Edward Valentine, John Warren's bond	£30
	4 days attendance	£1.4.0
1796	**CREDITS**	
	James Taylor's bond for Negro hire	£20.10
27 Dec	Cash rec'd of Col. Willis Wilson	£50

1797		
4 Feb	John Mitchel's bond for Negro hire	£8.5
	John Mitchel's bond for Negro hire	£3.13
	Cash rec'd Edward Valentine	£3
	John Warren's bond	£30
	Cash rec'd Joshua Oldner, late Overseer of the Poor, in settling his account	£16.17.10½
	Cash rec'd Goldsbury Hacket for his bond	£8.9.8

Elizabeth River Parish in account with John Wilkins

1796	**DEBITS**	
	Cash pd to Samuel Wilder for himself and 2 children from 1 Jun 1796 to 1 Oct 1796, in full	£5.7.4
Dec 27	Cash pd to Joshua Peaton for 3 months being in full to 1 Oct 1796	£1.16
	Cash pd to Mary Churnick for 3 months to 1 Oct 1796	£2.14
	Cash pd Mrs. Connoly & daughter from 1 Aug 1796 to 1 Dec 1796	£6.13.4
	Cash pd James Cooper for Dinah & Jonathan[8] Cooper's board for 2 months being in full to 1 Sep 1796	£6
1797		
10 Feb	Cash pd Mrs. Williams for Edward Driver's board for the year 1796 in full	£2.8
3 Oct	1 day attendance at Portsmouth at a meeting & ferriage	6s 7½p
24 Dec	1 day attendance at Portsmouth at a meeting & ferriage	6s 7½p
27 Dec	Ferriage on parish business	7½p
4 Jan	Hiring out Parish Negroes in Norfolk	6s
11 Jan	Taking bonds for the Parish Negroes	6s
7 Mar	2 days attendance in Portsmouth	12s
21 Mar	Cash pd Mr. Lemuel Denby for the use of the poor in his district	£19
	Cash pd Edward Valentine for his poor	£12
	Cash pd James Cooper for boarding Dinah & John Cooper in full to 1 Feb 1797	£15
	Cash pd Mrs. Conolly & daughter from 1 Dec 1796 to 1 Mar 1797	£5
1797	**CREDITS**	
	Cash rec'd of Mr. John Shield	£3
	Cash rec'd of Mr. Edward Valentine	£17.3.6

[8] He is listed as John in other accounts like this.

Elizabeth River Parish in account with Lemuel Denby

1796	**DEBITS**	
4 May	Cash pd Ann's 2 children *[Gumlinson?]*	£1.16
25 Jun	Attendance at Portsmouth & ferriage	6s 9p
2 Jul	Cash pd Ann Gumlinson for keeping 2 children	£3
4 Jul	Cash pd James Wilder for keeping John Jinkins	£2.8
29 Jul	Cash pd Abigail Cooper	6s
15 Aug	Cash pd James Grant for keeping Bridget Grant	£3.6
23 Aug	Cash pd John Cooper for keeping Frank Chatmond	£6
2 Sep	Cash pd John Grant for keeping Bridget Grant	£1.16
	Cash pd Edward Valentine for the behoof of Joseph Haymond for keeping Ed Jinkins	£4.10
	Cash pd Abigail Cooper	12s
	Attendance in Portsmouth & ferriage	6s 9p
	Cash pd for Malachi Denby's coffin & funeral charges to John Cooper	£2.2
17 Oct	Attendance at court & ferriage	6s 9p
	Cash pd John Grant, James Taylor's bond for keeping Bridget & Charles Cooper	£20.10
24 Dec	Attendance at Portsmouth & ferriage	6s 9p
27 Dec	Cash pd James Wilder for keeping John Ginkins	£5.7
29 Dec	Cash pd Joseph Haymond for Elizabeth Gurkins	£3
1797		
14 Jan	Cash pd Abigail Cooper	15s
	Attendance at hiring the Parish Negroes	6s
15 Jan	Cash pd John Cooper for keeping Frank Chatmond in part	£7.10
	Cash pd Mrs. Brewer's house rent	£1.17.6
	2 days attendance & ferriage	13s 6p
	Attendance at hiring the Parish Negroes	6s
	CREDITS	
	Cash rec'd William O'Grady in part Dr. Perry's bond	£7.10
	Cash rec'd Maximillian Herbert	£18.15
	James Taylor's bond	£20.10
	Cash rec'd of Edward Valentine	£17.3.6

1797 – 1798 Entries

Norfolk County in account with Andrew Kidd for Collection of the Poor Tax

DEBITS	
Balance due me at settlement with the former Overseer as collector for 1797	£35.5.3½
Cash pd William Marley per order Mr. Nimmo, Overseer of the Poor	£2.3.6
Cash pd William Plummer per order Mr. Watts, Overseer of the Poor	£2.12.1½

Cash pd Abram B. Cotton per order Mr. Watts, Overseer of the Poor	£1.10
Cash pd William Watts, Overseer of the Poor, at sundry payments	£60.13.6
Orders drawn by James Brown, Overseer of the Poor, amount paid sundry people	£94.10.08
Cash pd James Brown, Overseer of the Poor	£4.10
Cash pd John Pollick, Overseer of the Poor	£13.5.3
Cash pd Joseph Owens per order Overseer of the Poor	£4
Cash pd John Cooper per order Mr. Talbot	£7.5.3½
Cash pd William Taylor per order Mr. Brown	£1.0.3
Cash pd Ed Moore per order Mr. Brown	£2.5
Insolvents	£6.15
Commissions at 10%	£20.17.1¾
CREDITS	
Amount of Poor Tax arising from the collection of 1,854 tithables being the number taken per list for the Parishes of Portsmouth & Elizabeth River for the year 1798	£208.11.6

Norfolk County in account with James Warden for the Collection of the Poor Tax

1797	**DEBITS**	
	Cash pd Col. Butt, Overseer of the Poor, per receipt	£136.7
	Cash pd James Boushell, Overseer of the Poor, per receipt	£33.12
	Cash pd James Grimes, Overseer of the Poor, per receipt	£48.3
	Insolvents & errors	£10.4
	Commissions at 10%	£25.16
1797	**CREDITS**	
	By amount of Poor Tax arising from the collection of 1,724 tithables being the number taken per list for the St. Brides Parish for the year 1797	£258.12

Portsmouth Parish in account with James S. Mathews

1797	**DEBITS**	
	Cash pd Joseph Carter from 1 Nov to 1 Apr 1797	£3.18
	Cash pd Mathew Howard from 2 Nov to 2 Apr 1797	£3
	Cash pd Thomas Cherry from 21 Oct to 21 Feb 1797	£2.8
	Cash pd Elizabeth House from 20 Oct to 20 Mar 1797	£7.10
	Cash pd Stephen Makins for keeping Reuben Taylor 6 weeks 19 Oct 1796	£2.14
7 Jan	Cash pd Elizabeth Brown	6s
23 Jan	Cash pd Levina Hogwood	6s
	Cash pd Mary Combs from 2 Nov to 2 May 1797	£5.8
	Cash pd Elizabeth Wilkins for keeping Nelson Thornton from 13 Oct to 13 Apr	£5.18
	Cash pd Mary McClanan for keeping John & Peggy Harnage, orphans, from 17 Oct to 17 Mar 1797	£6

	Cash pd Thomas Wakefield for keeping William Hare, orphan, from 1 Jul to 1 Jan 1797	£3.12
	6 days attendance from Mar 1796 to Mar 1797	£1.16
1797	**CREDITS**	
27 Dec	Cash rec'd John Shield	£15
4 Feb	Cash rec'd John Shield in bonds for hire of the Parish Negroes	£11.18

Elizabeth River Parish in account Edward Valentine

1797	**DEBITS**	
12 Jan	Cash pd James Guy for his support from 3 Nov last to this day	£2.18.6
	Cash pd Mary Clemmons for her support from 12 Sep to this day	£3
	1 day attendance in Jun last	6s
	2 days attendance at Oct Court last & ferriage	15s
	Cash let Mr. Conley have	12s
Mar	Cash pd Mr. Shield part of John Warren's bond	£3
	Cash pd Dr. Starke his account for attending the poor of the parish for the year 1796	£18.15.9
	Cash pd John Warren's account for rent of 2 plantations for poor people for the year 1796	£8
	Cash pd J. McDonnel for burying C. Conoly	12s
	Cash pd in Jan last for a blanket for Negro Jasper belonging to ye parish	9s
	1 day attendance at Portsmouth 24 Dec last	6s
	1 day attendance in Jan last hiring the Parish Negroes	6s
	Cash pd Mr. Wilkins being part of ferry money	£17.3.6
	Cash pd Mr. Denby being part of ferry money	£17.3.6
	1 month board John Jones from 12 Oct to the 12 Nov last	15s
	1 day attendance at General Meeting	6s
1796	**CREDITS**	
3 Oct	Cash rec'd Mr. Shield	£3
	James Crawford's bond	£10
27 Dec	Cash rec'd Col. Wilson	£50
	A. Cowan's bond	£5.6
	John Warren's bond	£30

St. Brides Parish in account with Josiah Butt

1797	**DEBITS**	
15 Feb	Cash pd James Sikes	£6.0.3
17 Feb	Cash pd James Sikes	£1.2.4
	Cash pd John Dickens 30 Dec 1796	£2.16.9
	Cash pd John Dickens	14s
10 Jan	Cash pd John Dickens	£2.18

27 Feb	Cash pd John Dickens	£3.10.6
11 Mar	Coffin for said Dickens and digging grave	18s
11 Feb	Cash pd Abiah Creekmur	£3.12
2 Feb	Cash pd Zachariah Douge	£3.18
20 Mar	Cash pd Zachariah Douge	£3.2
8 Feb	Cash pd David & John Dennis	£3.19.3
5 Mar	Cash pd David & John Dennis	£3.18.6
27 Jan	Cash pd Old Free Punch	£1.1.5
	Cash pd Old Free Joe	£1.1.5
	Cash pd James Sikes from 6 Apr to 15 Aug	£9.9.5
	Cash pd Frances Boush 15 Aug	£3
	Cash pd Zachariah Douge from 28 Apr to 13 Sep	£15.11.3
	Cash pd Tim J. Wood for keeping David & John Dennis from 25 Mar to 6 Apr	£3.15.9
	Cash pd Tim J. Wood for funeral charges David Dennis	£1.26
	Cash pd Tim J. Wood for keeping John Dennis from Apr 6 to Aug 15	£3
13 Sep	Cash pd Rachel Burgess, a poor woman	£2.16
	Cash pd Abiah Creekmur from 10 May to 15 Aug	£8.13
	Cash pd Amy Dickens from 25 May to 22 Sep	£8.17.2
	Cash pd Rebeccah Woodward (in Jun)	£2.5
	Orders drawn on James Warden	£27
	3 days attendance from Mar to Sep	18s
1797	**CREDITS**	
Jun	Cash rec'd of Col. Wilson	£50
	Cash rec'd of Col. Wilson	£24
	Orders drawn on James Warden, collector	£27

Portsmouth Parish in account with John Talbot

1795	**DEBITS**	
21 May	Order on George Dyson in favor Robert Berland for making coffin for Mr. Dowdall	12s
23 May	Order on George Dyson in favor Robert Berland for funeral charges	3s 9p
24 May	Cash pd John Spring at sundry times	£6.12.6
2 Jun	Cash pd Ann Harris at sundry times	£8.14.6
23 Jun	Cash pd Joseph Thompson for Milly Hazelgrove 3 weeks board	£1.4
24 Jun	Cash pd George Joliffe for keeping Rhody Mackie	£3.12
	Cash pd Hannah Pierce & 3 children	£9.5.9
26 Jun	Cash pd Hannah Culpeper (now dead)	£2.7.10
	Cash pd Sarah Welch sundry times	£7.4.7½
29 Jun	Cash pd Mary Millow	£4.5.6
	Cash pd Ann Wakefield for William Hare's orphan	8s
3 Jul	Cash pd Samuel Stafford for keeping Smith Stafford	£4.13
20 Sep	Cash pd George Townsend for keeping Wright Deans	£8.14.3½

1796		
19 Jan	Cash pd Mary Bowers for keeping Sarah Ivey	£3
25 Jan	Cash pd Mary Callahan for Elizabeth Griffin including coffin & funeral charges	£1.10.8
25 Feb	Cash pd John Deale for keeping Margaret Deale, orphan[9]	11s 3p
	Cash pd Mary Bental and 3 children	£2.4
1796		
	Cash pd Sarah Welch in full to 1 Apr 1796	£2.15.5½
	Cash pd George Townsend for keeping Wright Deans	5s 3p
29 Feb	Cash pd Samuel Stafford for keeping Smith Stafford	£4.16
30 Mar	Cash pd John Spring	£1.4
	Cash pd Elizabeth Rose, poor woman	6s
	Cash pd Hannah Pierce in full to 1 Apr	15s
1 Apr	Cash pd Ann Harris in full to 1 Apr	£1.5.6
	Cash pd John Deale for keeping Margaret Deale	12s
17 Apr	Cash pd Mary Bental and 3 children	12s
18 May	Cash pd George Townsend in full for Wright Deans to 1 Apr	£3.5.8
14 May	Cash pd Hannah Pierce in part for 1796	£1.13.3
16 May	Cash pd Mary Bental	£1.10
29 May	Cash pd Sarah Welch in part for 1796	£1.5.6
31 May	Cash pd George Townsend for Wright Deans for 1796	£3.5.8
23 Jun	Cash pd Elisha Smith, a poor man,	£1.5.6
	Cash pd John Spring in full to 1 Apr	£1.3.6
	Cash pd Mary Bowers in full for keeping Sarah Ivey to 1 Apr	£6
24 Jul	Cash pd Elizabeth Stafford in full for Smith Stafford to 1 Apr 1796	£2.11
	Cash pd Samuel Bufkin for keeping Milly Hazelgrove	£2.2
25 Jul	Cash pd George Joliffe for keeping Rhody Mackie to 1 Apr 1796	£2.2
	Cash pd Henry Pulling in full for keeping Lavina Ross to 1 Apr 1796	£1.7.6
	Cash pd Robert Hargroves for moving Margaret Tucker from Nansemond County to this county[10]	6s
24 Sep	Cash pd Hannah Pierce in part for 1796	£3.0.9
27 Sep	Cash pd Nathan Rose in part for Elizabeth Rose	£2.2
	Cash pd Sarah Welch in part for 1796	£1.10
	Cash pd George Townsend for Wright Deans 1796	£2.5.3
	Cash pd Mary Bental	£1.10
	Cash pd Ann Isdel in part for 1796	£1.16
	Cash pd John Spring in part for 1796	8s

[9] Often when a person of one surname is being paid to keep a person of the same surname, you can find a relationship.

[10] The counties were required to take back the poor who moved to another county but had not set up the required residency. You will see several examples in this book.

12 Oct	Cash pd Elizabeth Stafford for Smith Stafford in part	£2.13
16 Oct	Cash pd William Britton for keeping John Bunting	£5.16
27 Oct	Cash pd Mary Callahan sundry times	£2.0.4½
14 Nov	Cash pd John Jones for Elizabeth Ivey in full to 5 Mar 1796	£5
3 Dec	Cash pd Margaret Tucker for keeping Samuel Creekmur as per account	£2
	Cash pd Edward Moore for keeping Sarah Ives, orphan, in full to 5 Mar 1796	£7
	Cash pd John Bowers for keeping William Wingate in full to 1 Apr 1796	£2.18.4
13 Dec	Cash pd Elizabeth Stafford for keeping Smith Stafford in part for 1796	12s
28 Dec	Cash pd George Townsend for Wright Deans in part	£2.2
30 Dec	Cash pd John Spring in part for 1796	£1.4
1797		
5 Jan	Cash pd William Britton for keeping John Bunting	£2.8
6 Jan	Cash pd Hannah Pierce in part for 1796	£1.4
12 Jan	Cash pd Elizabeth Stafford for Smith Stafford	£1.1
14 Jan	Cash pd John Deale in part his account	£3.2
19 Jan	Cash pd Nathan Rose in part for Mary Bental	£1.16
	Cash pd John Graham for Ann Harris	£1.4
	Cash pd Mary Callahan in full for Thomas Griffin, orphan, to 1 Jan 1797	£2.19.7½
	Cash pd John Deale in part (omitted 4 Jun 1796)	£1.14
	Cash pd George Townsend a balance in full due from George Wainwright late overseer	£4.4
	5 days attendance	£1.10
1795	**CREDITS**	
21 May	Order on George Dyson in favor of Robert Borland for coffin for Mrs. Dowdal	12s
	Order on George Dyson in favor of Robert Borland for funeral for Mrs. Dowdal	3s 9p
	Cash rec'd from George Dyson	£9
15 Jun	Cash rec'd from George Dyson	£9
13 Aug	Cash rec'd from George Dyson	£4.10
	Cash rec'd from Willis Wilson	£4.10
21 Nov	Cash rec'd from George Dyson	£9
21 Dec	Cash rec'd from George Dyson	£9
1796		
18 Jan	Cash rec'd from George Dyson	£11
26 Mar	Cash rec'd from Willis Wilson	£21
14 May	Cash rec'd from Willis Wilson	£25.4
9 Jul	Cash rec'd from John Shield	£15
	Cash rec'd from John Shield	£30
	Cash rec'd from John Shield	£21

Portsmouth Parish in account with James S. Mathews

1797	**DEBITS**	
20 Mar	Cash pd Elizabeth House	£1.10
	Cash pd Patsey Scott for keeping John & Peggy Harnage to 17 May	£2.14
	Cash pd William Croker for keeping from *[blank]* Campbell to 29 Mar	£1.10
	Cash pd Thomas Cherry from 21 Feb to 21 Apr	£1.4
	Cash pd Joseph Carter from 1 Apr to 1 May	£1.10
	Cash pd Mathew Howard from 2 Apr to 2 May	£1.10
	Cash pd Elizabeth Wilkins for Nelson Thornton's orphan from 14 Apr to 2 May	18s
	Order in favor William Willey on A. Kidd, collector	12s
1 Jul	Order in favor Joseph Britton on A. Kidd, collector	15s
	Cash pd John Talbot Overseer of the Poor for his poor	£15.13
	Order on Andrew Kidd in favor Thomas Owens for keeping Polly Campbell from 6 Jul to 6 Sep	£2.14
	Cash pd Thomas Wakefield for keeping William Hare, orphan, from 1 Jan to 1 Sep	£2.16
	3 days attendance up to Sep	18s
1797	**CREDITS**	
21 Mar	Cash rec'd John Shield	£15
17 Apr	Cash rec'd Col. Wilson	£2.8
1 Jul	Cash rec'd Col. Wilson	£15.13
	Order on A. Kidd in favor William Willey	15s
	Order on A. Kidd in favor Joseph Britton	12s
	Order on A. Kidd in favor Thomas Owens for P. Campbell	£2.14

Elizabeth River Parish in account with Edward Valentine

	DEBITS	
	Bonds delivered to Mr. John Wilkins being part of the bonds rec'd of Joshua Oldner	£44.15
	Bonds delivered to Mr. Lemuel Denby	£15.10
	Bonds delivered to Mr. John Shield	£6.15
	Cash pd Mrs. Clemmonds in full for 4 months board Mrs. Riddle	£2.14
	Cash pd Henry Guy in part for the present year's board of J. Jones	£6
	Cash pd James Davis for one year board of Henry Davis up to Feb last	£9
	Cash pd Francis Reynolds for a coffin for C. Conoly	12s
	Cash pd R. Spratleyfor crying part the Parish Negroes at hiring present year	9s
Aug	Cash advance Mrs. Riddle for 5 months allowance to this day	£3.7.6
	Cash advance James Davis per order A. Kidd	£6

	Cash advance James Davis in part for this year's board of Henry Davis	£3
	Cash pd Mrs. Harvey for 1 month allowance	12s
Sep	1 day attendance at meeting Overseers of Poor	6s 9p
	1 month's allowance Mrs. Riddle up to the 26th instant paid for staples etc.	14s 3p
	Cash pd William Davis for advertising Will Snale when runaway	5s 6p
25 Sep	A month's allowance to Mrs. Harvey and children due 18th instant	12s
1797	**CREDITS**	
	Aforementioned bonds delivered to Messrs Shield, Wilkins & Denby which was rec'd from Joshua Oldner	£67
Mar	Cash rec'd of Mr. Wilkins	£12
Aug	Order on Mr. Kidd in favor of James Davis	£6

St. Brides Parish in account with James Grimes

1797	**DEBITS**	
	Cash pd Henry Creekmur	£12.2.4
	Cash pd Polly Hodges	£3
10 Aug	Cash pd James Creekmur, Sr.	£4.11.9
	Cash pd Betsey Creekmur	£3.13
7 Jun	Cash pd James Creekmur, Jr.	£2.8
19 Jul	Burying Henry McPherson	£1.7.9
	Cash pd James Holt, late overseer, being a balance due him at settling his account	£3.12.10½
	Cash pd James Boushell for his poor	£15
1797	**CREDITS**	
	Cash	£50

Portsmouth Parish in account with John Shield

1797	**DEBITS**	
8 Mar	Cash pd Mary Brown for orphan	6s
9 Mar	Cash pd William Willey	£1.4
21 Mar	Cash pd Mary Brown for orphans	6s
	Cash pd Joseph Carter	7s 6p
	Cash pd Hillary Cherry	£1.16
	Cash pd John Talbot	£24
	Cash pd James S. Mathews	£15
24 Mar	Cash pd Margaret Cassel	18s
28 Mar	Cash pd Lydia Sykes	£2.2
30 Mar	Cash pd James Taylor for E. Rose	6s
31 Mar	Cash pd Stephen Anderson	£1.4
3 Apr	Cash pd William Willey	£1.6.6
7 Apr	Cash pd Mary Brown	£1
5 May	Cash pd Cloe Deale & child	£1.1

	Cash pd Mary Brown & child	16s
8 May	Cash pd Stephen Anderson	12s 4p
11 May	Cash pd Jeremiah Rutter shoes for Jo. Carter	4s
	Cash pd William Willey from A. Kidd	£1.10
20 May	Cash pd James Woodward for account in full	£8.11
23 May	Cash pd Margaret Cadenhead	12s
5 Jun	Cash pd Stephen Anderson	6s
7 Jun	Cash pd William Willey from A. Kidd	£1.4
24 Jun	Cash pd David Richardson for Cloe Deale	£2.2
	Cash pd Eliza Pierce, blind woman	12s
	Cash pd James Taylor for Elizabeth Rose	£4.10.9
28 Jun	Cash pd Mary Brown	£1.1
6 Jul	Cash pd Elizabeth Peak	12s
18 Jul	Cash pd Margaret Cassel	12s
26 Jul	Cash pd Dr. Leigh for attending poor	£8.3.6
15 Aug	Cash pd Margaret Cassel	6s
28 Aug	Cash pd Stephen Anderson	6s
26 Sep	3 days attendance	18s
	Cash pd James Lowe for Jo. Carter in Mar omitted	£1.16
1797	**CREDITS**	
21 Mar	Cash rec'd Col. Willis Wilson	£50
11 May	Cash rec'd of A. Kidd, collector	£6.4.2
20 May	By O'Conner rec'd his bond for Negro hire	£6.15
	By James Woodward rec'd his bond for Negro hire	£1.10
28 Jun	Cash rec'd Col. Willis Wilson	£10.7
24 Jul	Cash rec'd J. Mordecai for his bond for Negro hire	£7.9

Elizabeth River Parish in account with John Wilkins

1797	**DEBITS**	
	Cash pd Mrs. Churnick from 1 Oct 1796 to 10 Jan in full	£3
	Cash pd Joshua Peaton for 3 months to 1 Jan 1797	£1.16
	Cash pd Samuel Wilder for himself & 2 children from 1 Oct 1796 to 15 May 1797	£10.1.3
10 Jul	Cash pd Mrs. Denny, a poor woman, with 3 children	12s
	Cash pd Mrs. Harvey, one of the poor, in Mr. Valentine's district	3s
9 Aug	Cash pd Mrs. Conoly in full up to 15 Jul	£4.10
	Cash pd Hilliary Snale for Samuel Wilder's coffin	£1
1 Sep	Cash pd Mr. J. Conway for John Kilgrow's orphans board for the year 1796 in full	£7.4
	4 days attendance at the meetings of the Overseers in Portsmouth & ferriage	£1.7

1797	**CREDITS**	
21 Mar	Cash rec'd Col. Wilson	£50
5 May	Cash rec'd Dr. Taylor in part his bond for the Parish Negroes	£4.10
5 Jul	Cash rec'd Benjamin Welcome on his bond	£2.8
4 Aug	Cash rec'd John West in part his bond for hire Negro	£2
	Cash rec'd Thomas Brown in part his bond for hire Negro	£2.8
24 Aug	Cash rec'd of Mr. A. Kidd, collector	£15.19.2
	Cash rec'd Mr. Richard Gibbons in part his bond for hire one of the Parish Negroes	£7.19

Elizabeth River Parish in account with Lemuel Denby

1797	**DEBITS**	
27 Mar	Cash pd John Cooper for keeping Frankey Chatmond	£12
	Cash pd James Wilder for John Jinkins	£2.2
28 Mar	Cash pd George Heaney for Mary Langley	£1.16.6
	Cash pd Joseph Haymond for keeping Elizabeth Jinkins	£1.4
7 Apr	Cash pd Henry Brag for Ann Tumlinson's rent	£5
20 May	Cash pd Ann Denby[11] being part of Malachi Denby's claim	£1.10
30 May	Cash pd John Read	18s
10 Jul	Cash pd John Read	£1.1
24 Jul	Cash pd John Cooper for keeping Frankey Chatmond in part	£3.12
5 Aug	Cash pd Joseph Haymond for keeping Elizabeth Jinkins in part	£1.10
10 Aug	Cash pd John Read	18s
	Cash pd James Wilder for keeping John Jinkins	£1.4
	Cash pd Joseph Haymond	£1.10
	Cash pd John Read	12s
15 Sep	Cash pd John Cooper for keeping Frankey Chatmond	£2.8
22 Sep	Cash advanced John Read	12s
	3 days attendance & ferriage at Portsmouth at Meeting of the Overseers of the Poor	£1.0.3
1797	**CREDITS**	
21 Mar	Cash rec'd of John Wilkins	£19
5 Aug	Cash rec'd of Mr. A. Kidd, collector	9s 6p
9 Sep	Cash rec'd in part of Brown's bond	2s 8p

11 There's a possibility that Malachi has died and his wife is collecting money owed his estate since Malachi married Ann Tigner in 1793 (Sharon Gable and Truitt Bonney, *Norfolk County Virginia (extant) Marriage Bonds 1706-1850* (Suffolk, Virginia: privately published, 2015), p 75.).

Portsmouth Parish in account with John Talbot

1797	DEBITS	
21 Mar	Cash pd William Britton for keeping John Bunting	£3.12
29 Mar	Cash pd Absalom Bruce due by George Wainwright late Overseer of the Poor	£1.5.9
	Cash pd Elizabeth Stafford for keeping Smith Stafford due by George Wainwright late Overseer of the Poor	£2.10
4 Apr	Cash pd Nathan Rose for keeping Elizabeth Rose, very sickly	£2.8
	Cash pd Henry Pullen for keeping Levina Rose in part	£3
6 Apr	Cash pd Hannah Pearce, a poor woman, and 2 children	£2.7.3
26 Apr	Cash pd George Townsend, a poor man	£1.16
10 May	Cash pd Mary Bowers in part for 1796	£9
	Cash pd Ann Harris in full up to 1797 from 1 Apr	£5
21 Jun	Cash pd Henry Pullen for keeping Levina Rose in full up to 5 Apr	£2.8
30 Jun	Cash pd Stephen Anderson, a poor man	18s 9p
7 Jul	Cash pd Robert Bowers for John Spring, a lame man, in part for 1797	£3.7.6
25 Jul	Cash pd Mary Turner, a poor woman	3s 9p
	Cash pd Henry Thompson for keeping Austin Spain, very sickly, in part	6s
28 Aug	Cash pd Margaret Tucker for keeping Sally Powell, very lame, to this date	£6.6
	Cash pd Sarah Welch, a poor woman	6s 3p
1797		
	Order on A. Kidd, collector, in favor Elizabeth Stafford for keeping Smith Stafford, one of the poor	£5
	Order on A. Kidd, collector, in favor John Deale for keeping Margaret Deale, an orphan, in full for the year 1796	£2.14.9
	Order on A. Kidd, collector, in favor L. Godwin	£2.8
	Order on A. Kidd, collector, in favor Sarah Welch in full up to 1 Apr	£7.4.6
	Order on A. Kidd, collector, in favor George Townsend for keeping Wright Deans in full up to 1 Apr	£7.12
	Order on A. Kidd, collector, in favor William Britton for keeping John Buntin in full to the 1 Jan 1797	£6.4
	Order on A. Kidd, collector, in favor Ben Bolton for boarding Mary Campbell in full	£3
	Order on A. Kidd, collector, in favor Ben Bolton for boarding Mary Bental & 2 children in full to 1 Apr	£6.14
	Order on A. Kidd, collector, in favor David Eastwood for keeping Austin Spain 2 months, very sickly	£2.8
	Order on A. Kidd, collector, in favor Mary Bowers for keeping 2 orphan children in full to 1 Mar	£9
	Order on A. Kidd, collector, in favor Elizabeth Stafford for keeping Smith Stafford in full to 1 Apr	£8.14

	Cash pd Archibald Bruce for keeping William Farley from 10 Feb 1796 to 10 Feb 1797	£12
	Cash pd for boarding and sending Sarah Powell to the doctor	15s
	Cash pd for Robert Bowers for keeping John Spring, omitted 20 Mar	7s 6p
	Cash pd for Hannah Pierce, one of the poor	7s 6p
1 May	Order on A. Kidd, collector, in favor Elizabeth Stafford for keeping Smith Stafford in part	£5
5 May	Order on A. Kidd, collector, in favor John Deale for keeping Margaret Deale, an orphan, in full for 1796	£2.14.9
26 May	Order on A. Kidd, collector, in favor Lankford Godwin	£2.8
16 Jun	Order on A. Kidd, collector, in favor Sarah Welch	£7.4.6
20 Jun	Order on A. Kidd, collector, in favor George Townsend for Wright Deans in full up to 1 Apr 1797	£7.12
	Order on A. Kidd, collector, in favor William Britton for keeping John Buntin in full to the 1 Jan 1797	£6.4
	Order on A. Kidd, collector, in favor Benjamin Bolton for Mary Cammel in full	£3
	Order on A. Kidd, collector, in favor Mary Bental, a poor woman, & 2 children in full	£6.14
20 Jun	Order on A. Kidd in favor Ned Moore for Ann Ivey, orphan, in full to 1 Mar 1797,	£8
7 Jul	Order on A. Kidd in favor Samuel Bufkin for Milly Hazelgrove	£1.19
1 Aug	Order on A. Kidd in favor Elizabeth Ellis for John Griffis, orphan, from Jan 1796 to Jan 1797, now dead	£6
	Order on A. Kidd in favor Archibald Bruce for William Farley 6 months up to 10 Feb 1797	£6
	Order on A. Kidd in favor Richard Powell for John Powell 6 months, lame, up to 1 Feb 1797	£5.8
3 Aug	Order on A. Kidd, collector, in favor George Townsend for keeping Wright Deans for 3 months up to 1 Apr 1797	£3
	Order on A. Kidd, collector, in favor Ann Harris for keeping Ann Isdel 3 months up to Apr	£2.10
19 Aug	Order on A. Kidd, collector, in favor Robert Bowers for keeping John Spring this present year	£1.4
	Order on A. Kidd, collector, in favor Lankford Godwin	£2.8
7 Mar	Cash rec'd Mr. John Shield	£7.10
31 May	Order on A. Kidd in favor of David Eastwood for keeping Austin Spain 2 months	£2.8
20 Jun	Order on A. Kidd in favor of Mary Bowers for 2 orphan children in full to Mar	£9
	Order on A. Kidd in favor Elizabeth Stafford for Smith Stafford in full to 1 Apr 1797	£8.14
	Order on A. Kidd in favor Ned Moore for Ann Ivey in full up to 1797	£8

7 Jul	Order on A. Kidd in favor Samuel Bufkin for Milly Hazelgrove in full to 1797	£1.19
1 Aug	Order on A. Kidd in favor Elizabeth Ellis for John Griffis, orphan, up to Jan 1797 in full	£6
	Order on A. Kidd in favor Archibald Bruce for William Farley 6 months up to 10 Feb 1797	£6
	Order on A. Kidd in favor Richard Powell for John Powell 6 months, very lame	£5.8
3 Aug	Order on A. Kidd in favor of George Townsend for Wright Deans 3 months from 1 Apr	£3
	Order on A. Kidd in favor of Ann Harris for Ann Isdel for 3 months from 1 Apr	£2.10
19 Aug	Order on A. Kidd in favor of Robert Bowers for John Spring this present year in part	£1.4
	Order on A. Kidd in favor Lankford Godwin	£2.8
	3 days attendance	18s
	CREDITS	
21 Mar	Cash rec'd of John Shield	£24
20 Jun	Cash rec'd of Andrew Kidd	£3.6
	Cash rec'd of James S. Mathews	£15.13

St. Brides Parish in account with James Boushell

1797	**DEBITS**	
20 Feb	1 bushel corn advanced Richard Cain, one of the poor	6s
2 Mar	1 bushel corn advanced Richard Cain, one of the poor	6s
6 Mar	2 days attendance on the Overseers for the Poor	12s
13 Mar	Cash pd Richard Cain for support until 13 Apr	12s
21 Mar	1 day attendance on meeting	6s
	Cash pd Frances Boushell per order	£15.13
13 Apr	Cash pd Richard Cain for support til 13 May	12s
	Cash pd Richard Cain's child for support	6s
	Cash pd Richard Cain's support til 13 Jun	12s
13 Jun	Cash pd Richard Cain's child	6s
	Cash pd Richard Cain & child for support til 13 Jul	18s
13 Jul	Cash pd Richard Cain & child for support til 13 Aug	18s
	Cash pd Richard Cain & child for support til 13 Sep	18s
13 Sep	Cash pd Richard Cain & child for support til 13 Nov	12s
2 Jun	2 bushels corn advanced William Griggs for one of the poor	12s
	Cash to William Griggs	8s
	2 bushels corn advanced William Griggs for one of the poor	12s
	Cash to William Griggs for one of the poor	8s
2 Aug	Cash to William Griggs	5s
23 Sep	2 days attendance on the Overseers for the Poor	12s

1797	CREDITS	
6 Mar	Cash rec'd	£1.15
21 Mar	Cash rec'd	18s
7 Aug	Cash rec'd from James Grimes	£15.13
	Cash rec'd	£6
23 Sep	Cash rec'd from James Warden	£24

Portsmouth Parish in account with James S. Mathews

1797	DEBITS	
	Cash pd Zebro Kellum 3 months up to 27 Dec	18s
	Cash pd Elizabeth Wilkins 3 months up to 27 Dec	18s
	Cash pd William Smith 1 month up to 2 Oct	£1.10
	Cash pd Mary Clements 3 months up to 27 Dec	18s
	Cash pd Dorcas Day agreeable to an order of the Overseers	£6
	Cash pd Patsey Scott 3 months for keeping John and Peggy Harnage up to 17 Feb 1798	£4.10
	Cash pd Mathew Howard 3 months up to 2 Feb	£4.10
	Cash pd Elizabeth House 2 months up to 20 Jan	£3.12
	Cash pd Mary Britton 4 months up to 2 Feb	£4.4
	Cash pd Ann Cherry 3 months up to 21 Jan	£2.5
	Cash pd Elizabeth Wilkins for keeping Nelson Thornton 3 months up to 13 Feb 1798	£2.14
	Cash pd Joseph Carter 2 months up to 1 Jan	£3
	Order on A. Kidd in favor of Thomas Owens for keeping Polly Campbell 14 Oct	£1.7
	Cash pd Elizabeth Brown 3 months up to 6 Jan	£1.16
	2 days attendance	12s
1797	**CREDITS**	
14 Oct	Order on A. Kidd in favor of Thomas Owens	£1.7
	Cash rec'd of John Shield	£10.10
1798		
3 Jan	Cash rec'd of Col. W. Wilson	£24
	Cash rec'd from William Walls	£1.17.6

Portsmouth Parish in account with John Shield

1797	DEBITS	
26 Sep	Cash pd Thomas Deale	12s
	Cash pd James S. Mathews for his poor	£10.10
	Cash pd John Wilkins for his poor	£23.9.6
	Cash pd John Talbot for his poor	£15
	Cash pd Col. Butt for his poor	£9
28 Sep	Cash pd Mary Brown	18s
30 Sep	Cash pd Stephen Anderson	18s
6 Oct	Cash pd Dr. Leigh in full of his salary up to this day	£3.16.6
	Cash pd George Capron for sundries supplied the poor on Deep Creek	£4.18.6

18 Oct	Cash pd Elizabeth Peak	9s
19 Oct	Cash pd Margaret Cassel	9s
3 Nov	Cash pd Thomas Deale	9s 9p
18 Nov	Cash pd Elizabeth Peak	9s
11 Dec	Cash pd Margaret Cassel	9s
1798		
6 Jan	Cash pd Stephen Anderson	£1.10
13 Jan	Cash pd Morris Damron & wife	18s
18 Jan	Cash pd Mary Brown & child	7s 6p
	Cash pd William Plummer for Fanny Peake	12s
26 Jan	Cash pd Stephen Anderson	£1.4
30 Jan	Cash pd Morris Damron	£1.10
31 Jan	Cash pd Elizabeth Peak	18s
3 Feb	Cash pd Margaret Cadenhead	6s
13 Feb	Cash pd Margaret Cassel	18s
	2 days attendance	12s
	Cash pd James Brown, Overseer of the Poor	£7.10
	Cash pd Dr. Leigh part of his salary	£1.10
	Cash pd Elizabeth Peak in Mar *(omitted)*	6s
	Expenses 10 days collecting bonds etc.	£3
1797	**CREDITS**	
26 Sep	Cash rec'd of Col. W. Wilson	£70.10
1798		
	Dr. O'Grady's bond	£17

Portsmouth Parish in account with John Talbot

	DEBITS	
7 Sep	Order on A. Kidd in favor Henry Thompson for keeping Austin Spain 3 months	£3.12
2 Oct	Order on A. Kidd in favor George Townsend for keeping Wright Deans 3 months	£3.2
	Order on A. Kidd in favor Sarah Ellis for Thomas Griffis 6 months	£3
6 Oct	Order on A. Kidd in favor William Britton for keeping John Bunting 6 months	£10
14 Oct	Order on A. Kidd in favor John Bowers, administrator of George Wainwright,[12] being part of a balance due said estate	£4.1.2½
30 Oct	Cash pd Benjamin Boulton for boarding Mary Millow and her funeral charges	£2.11.6
31 Oct	Cash pd Hannah Pierce	7s
	Cash pd Henry Pullen for keeping Levina Rose	£1.18.4

[12] An admin bond was issued to John Bowers dated 19 Oct 1795 for $7,000 as the widow relinquished her right to administer in favor of Bowers (Sharon Gable and Truitt Bonney, *Norfolk County Virginia (extant) Administrator Bonds 1711-1850* (Suffolk, Virginia: privately published, 2008), p 156.). Wainwright was an Overseer in the Portsmouth Parish.

	Cash pd Robert Bowers in favor of John Spring	£1.6.4
15 Dec	Cash pd Margaret Tucker for keeping Sarah Powell 3½ months	£4.4
	Cash pd Mary Bental per A. Kidd	12s
	Cash pd Richard Powell per A. Kidd	14s 3p
1798		
5 Jan	Cash pd George Townsend	5s
	Cash pd Sarah Powell for keeping Sarah Powell 3 months 15 Dec 1797 to 15 Dec 1798	£3.12
22 Mar	3 days attendance	18s
1797	**CREDITS**	
26 Sep	Cash rec'd John Shield for the poor	£15
	Order on A. Kidd in favor of Henry Thompson	£3.12
2 Oct	Order on A. Kidd in favor of George Townsend	£3.2
	Order on A. Kidd in favor of Sarah Ellis	£3
6 Oct	Order on A. Kidd in favor of William Britton	£10
14 Oct	Order on A. Kidd in favor of John Bowers	£4.1.2½
	Cash pd Mary Bental	12s
	Cash pd Richard Powell	14s 3p
1798		
	Cash rec'd A. Kidd, collector	15s
Jun	Cash rec'd A. Kidd, collector	13s 6p
	Cash rec'd Andrew Kidd per order James Brown	£9.0.11

Elizabeth River Parish in account with Edward Valentine

1797	**DEBITS**	
25 Sep	1 day attendance	6s
27 Oct	Cash pd Mrs. Harvey 1 month's allowance	12s
	Cash pd Mrs. Riddle 1 month's allowance	13s 6p
18 Nov	Cash pd Mrs. Harvey 1 month's allowance to 17 Nov	12s
2 Dec	Cash pd William Bird	6s
	Cash pd Mrs. Riddle up to 26 Nov	13s 6p
	Cash pd Mrs. Riddle up to 26 Nov 1797 to 26 Feb 1798	£2.0.6
	Cash advanced Mrs. Harvey from 17 Nov to 17 Mar 1798	£2.8
	Cash pd William Bird	10s 6p
	Cash pd Mrs. Gordon for keeping Tillah Fisher while sick in 1796	£4
	1 day attendance at Dec Court	6s
	2 days in hiring Parish Negroes	12s
1798	Cash pd Henry Guy	£3
	Cash pd drayman for carrying 2 corpse to the church yard	1s 6p
22 Mar	1 day attendance	6s
	Cash pd William Row for 2 coffins for 2 people by name of Crab	£1.4

2 Apr	Cash pd Henry Guy in full for keeping John Jones to 1 Jan last	£2
	A bond paid Dr. Starke for his attending the poor of Elizabeth River Parish last year	£19.14.3
	Cash advanced to Mrs. Riddle for a month's allowance to 26 Mar last	13s 6p
	Cash pd David Cooper for necessaries	4s 7½p
May	A. Campbell's bond paid to James Marley in part for keeping John Jones for the present year	£6.5
1797	**CREDITS**	
	Cash rec'd Andrew Kidd, collector	£5.17.10¼
Oct	Cash rec'd John Williams, Overseer of the Poor	£7.4
Feb	Cash rec'd John Williams, Overseer of the Poor	£7
Apr	Cash quarter rec'd James Marley's bond	£2.15
	Cash rec'd of Mrs. Street's bond	£2
	Cash rec'd of Mr. Graves' bond	£6.7.2
	Cash rec'd of H. Durant's bond	£2.10.9
	R. Gibbon's bond paid Dr. Starke	£18
	A. Campbell's bond paid James Marley	£6.5

Elizabeth River Parish in account with John Wilkins

1797	**DEBITS**	
	Cash pd Mrs. Conolly at sundry times up to 15 Feb 1798	£7
	Cash gave Mr. Bird, an object	3s
26 Sep	Cash pd Lemuel Denby for the use of the Poor of Elizabeth River Parish	£9
	Cash pd Edward Valentine for his poor	£7.4.0
20 Nov	Cash pd Mary Churnick to 1 Mar 1797	£1.10
	Cash pd Mrs. Wilder for her children's board to 1 Feb 1798	£5.13.4
	Cash pd James Cooper for Dinah & John Cooper in full to 1 Sep 1797	£20
1798		
6 Jan	Cash a bond Mr. Lemuel Denby in part of what the Negroes hired for 1797	£41.12
8 Jan	Cash gave Tom Wheeler, a poor object	3s
	Cash pd John Waddell for Tom Wheeler's coffin & other expenses	£1.5
	Cash pd John Connoway for John Citgres *[?]* board in full for 1797	£7.10
	Cash pd William Miller for Judah Cones' coffin	12s
	Cash pd Mrs. Wilkins in part for Nancy Dunton's board	£4.10
	My service hiring out the Parish Negroes and taking bonds	12s
10 Feb	Cash pd Edward Valentine for his poor	£7
	2 days attendance	12s

1797	**CREDITS**	
26 Sep	Cash rec'd of Mr. Shield in Portsmouth	£23.9.6
7 Oct	Cash rec'd of Mr. Andrew Kidd, collector	£1.10
	Cash rec'd on Mrs. Cordill's bond for Negro hire for 1797, being in part	£3
1798		
	Amount of Mr. Bennet's bond rec'd in full for 1797	£3.1
11 Jan	Amount of Mr. Gibbon's bond for hire Billy Pew for 1797	£10.11
	Amount of Benjamin Welcome's bond for hire Betsey Pew rec'd in full for the year 1797	£7.3
30 Jan	Cash rec'd of Dr. Taylor for the hire Joseph for 1797 in full	£13
	Cash rec'd of on West's bond for hire for the year 1797	£6
	Cash rec'd of on Mr. Brown's bond for Negro hire for 1797	£4.19
	Bonds Lemuel Denby	£41.12

Elizabeth River Parish in account with Lemuel Denby

1797	**DEBITS**	
	Cash pd Ann Denby in full	9s 7½p
8 Nov	Cash pd John Read	12s
14 Nov	Cash pd John ~~Jenkins~~ for keeping John Jenkins in part	18s
22 Nov	Cash pd John Grant for keeping Charles Cooper by order	£4.4
1798		
6 Jan	Bond paid John Grant for keeping Bridget Grant in full	£12
	1 day attendance hiring Parish Negroes	6s
	Cash pd for black bonds	3s
24 Jan	Cash pd for paid Selah Wilder for keeping for keeping John Jenkins	£1.6
1 Feb	Cash pd for paid John Cooper for keeping Frankey Chatmond	£6.3
	Order on Mr. Kidd in favor Joseph Hayman	£4.16
22 Mar	1 day attendance a meeting & ferriage	6s 9p
2 Apr	Cash pd Selah Wilder for keeping for keeping John Jenkins in part	12s
1 May	Cash pd Mrs. Elizabeth Wormsley for keeping 3 of Jenkins' children per order meeting	£22
9 May	Cash pd John Read	£4.6
	Cash pd Upshur Colony by order of the meeting	£3.10.6
1797	**CREDITS**	
26 Oct	Cash rec'd from John Wilkins	£9
24 Nov	Cash rec'd from Andrew Kidd	£1.4

1798		
6 Jan	Bonds	£12
	Cash rec'd in part from George Casson's bond	£3.6
	Order on Andrew Kidd in favor of J. Hayman	£4.16
	John Warren's bond for the year 1797	£20
	Balance of George Casson's bond 1797	£4.6
	Nicholas Booze's bond	£2

St. Brides Parish in account with James Grimes Overseer of the Poor

1797	**DEBITS**	
17 Oct	Cash pd James Williams for keeping William Oakley 2 months	£4.16
11 Nov	Cash pd James Creekmur, Sr.	£1.10.7
19 Nov	Cash pd James Creekmur, Jr.	£2.8
2 Dec	Cash pd Holly Hodges	£1.10
9 Dec	Cash pd James Creekmur, Sr.	£1.1.7
	Cash pd Benjamin Butt for keeping Dinah Banks' child	£1.4
	Cash pd Henry Creekmur	4s 10½p
	Cash pd James Creekmur, Jr.	£2.8
	Cash pd Benjamin Butt	£1.16
	Cash pd James Creekmur, Sr.	£3
	Cash pd James Casteel	12s
1798		
	Cash pd Henry Creekmur	£1.5.10
22 Mar	3 days attendance	18s
1 Jun	Cash pd James Creekmur, Sr.	£3.4
	Cash pd Mary Hodges for keeping her child	£2.10
19 Mar	Cash paid Jordan Marchant	£8.2
1797	**CREDITS**	
	Cash rec'd from James Warden, collector	£33
	Cash rec'd from James Warden, collector	£4.16
	Cash rec'd from James Warden, collector	£2.5

St. Brides Parish in account with Josiah Butt Overseer

1797	**DEBITS**	
7 Oct	Cash pd James Sykes for 2 months	£6
	Cash pd Abiah Creekmur	£6
15 Oct	Cash pd Timothy Wood	£1.4
16 Dec	Cash pd Stephen Nichols for keeping Free Punch one year	£5
27 Dec	Cash pd Edward Jones for keeping Sookey Boushell	£3
1798		
19 Jan	Cash pd Zachariah Douge	£4.10
	Cash pd Thomas Corprew for keeping Free Joe	£4.17
22 Jan	Cash pd William Hall, Sr. for keeping 2 of the poor 3 years	£57.10

	Cash pd Thomas Woodward for keeping Charles and Lovey Woodward, two orphans	£2
	Cash pd Francis Boush	£6
	Cash pd Joel Gammon for J. Hodges	£4.18
	Cash pd Amy Dickens	£2.2.9
22 Mar	1 day attendance	6s
	2 days attendance	12s
1797	**CREDITS**	
	Amount of orders drawn on James Warden, collector, for 1797	£98.19

The Overseers of the Poor for Norfolk County in Account with Andrew Kidd, Collector of the Poor Tax

1797	**DEBITS**	
	Sundry moneys paid the poor in the district of Mr. James S. Mathews, Overseer of the Poor	£70.2
	Sundry moneys paid Mr. John Talbot, Overseer of the Poor	£139.18.6
	Cash pd John Shield Esq	£6.4.2
	Cash pd John Millow per order	£5.14
	Cash pd Mr. John Wilkins, Overseer of the Poor	£15.19.2
	Cash pd William Marley per order Overseer of the Poor	£1.10
	Cash pd Mr. Lemuel Denby, Overseer of the Poor	£9.6
	Cash pd Joseph Hayman per order	£4.16
	Cash pd Mr. Edward Valentine, Overseer of the Poor	£11.17.10¼
	Cash pd Mr. Lemuel Denby, Overseer of the Poor	£1.4
	Cash pd Alexander Love per order	£1.16
	Cash pd John Bowers in part of his claim vs the Parish	£4.1.2½
	Insolvents	£11.2
	Commission at 10%	£28.18.4¾
	Salary as clerk 3 years	£18
1797	**CREDITS**	
	Collection of the 1,928 tithes being the number taken per list for the Parish of Portsmouth & Elizabeth River for the year 1797	£289.4
	Cash rec'd from Mr. Shield being 1 year's salary as clerk	£6

Norfolk County in Account Current with Richard Webb for the Collection of the Poor Tax

DEBITS	
Cash pd Mr. Jordan Marchant	£141.9
Cash pd Mr. William Bartee	£34.9.3
Constables 6 tax free	13s 6p
Insolvents 35	£3.18.9
Commissions at 10%	£19.12.3
Collection of 1,779 tithables being the number taken for the year 1798	£200.2.9

1798 – 1799 Entries

St. Brides Parish in account with William Bartee Overseer of the Poor

DEBITS	
Cash pd for keeping Henry Creekmur 20 Mar 1798 to 26 Jun 1800	£32.8
Cash pd James Creekmur 1 Jun 1798 until 1 Sep 1800	£32.8
Cash pd Mary Hodges for keeping 3 children from 4 Sep 1798 to 4 Oct 1800	£25
Cash pd Polly Hodges per order for keeping an orphan child up to 19 Feb 1800	£3.15
Cash pd Ann Parsons for keeping 3 children from 1 Jul 1799 to 1 Sep 1800	£14
Cash pd George Ferguson for 4 Sep 4 1799 to 4 Feb 1800	£6
Cash pd Caleb Butt for 1 Nov 1799 to 1 Feb 1800 (discharged)	£3.12
Cash pd Bridget Pierce for keeping William Creekmur 2 months	£1.16
Cash pd Solomon Charlton for making his coffin	12s
Cash pd Ferebee Messer for keeping 2 children from 1 Apr 1800 to 1 Oct 1800	£5
Cash pd Dr. Harding amount of his bill	£1.16.6
Cash pd Malachi Butt for removing Mr. Bright out of state	£1.10
Cash pd for conveying one of the poor to Dr. Harding	12s
Cash pd 14 days on business	£4.4
CREDITS	
Cash rec'd from Richard Webb, collector	£34.9.3
Cash rec'd from James Warden, collector	£4.10
Cash rec'd from John Butt, collector	£96.11.8

Elizabeth River Parish in account with John Wilkins Overseer of Poor

1798	DEBITS	
23 Mar	1 day attendance at a meeting of the Overseers of the Poor at Mr. John Mushrow's	6s
24 Mar	Cash pd Mrs. Wilkins, in part, for Nancy Dunton's board 1797	15s
	Cash pd Mrs. Connoly in full to 15 May 1798	£3

Apr	Bond pd James Cooper, viz for hire of one of the Parish Negroes for 1798, being in full for keeping Dinah & John Cooper to the 1 Jan 1798	£10
	Bond pd Mrs. Wilkins being in full for Nancy Dunton's board up to 1 Jun 1798	£9
24 Aug	Cash pd Mr. Gersham Nimmo for the use of the poor	£7.1
1798	**CREDITS**	
	Cash rec'd on a bond of Richard Gibbons for Negro hire for the year 1797	£6
Apr	Bonds rec'd of Mr. Edward Valentine for Negro hire for 1798	£19
24 Aug	Cash rec'd of Captain Oldner for Negro hire for the year 1797	£7.1
	Cash rec'd of John Holland	3s 8p

Elizabeth River Parish in account with Edward Valentine

1798	DEBITS	
Jul	Hager Johnson's account settled as per order of the Overseers in March last	£14.12.6
	Cash pd Hager Johnson for keeping a small child Becky the last year	£2
	1 day attendance	6s
	CREDITS	
Jul	The amount of Billy (Hager's son) and Betsey Pugh settled with Hager Johnson as per receipt	£15.18
	The amount of Billy (Hager's son) and Betsey Pugh settled with Hager Johnson of William Graves	£6.6

St. Brides Parish in account with Jordan Marchant

1798	DEBITS	
Jun	1 day attendance	6s
7 Jul	Cash pd Edward Jones for keeping Mrs. Boushell	£11.17
10 Jul	1 day attendance	6s
19 Jul	Cash pd Daniel Shirley per order	£6.18
15 Jul	Cash pd James Sikes per receipt	£7.10
2 Aug	Cash pd Mary Creekmur per receipt	£7.2.6
2 Sep	Cash pd Zach Douge per receipt	£7.10
	Cash pd Thomas Messer per receipt	£3.12
	Cash pd Francis Boush per receipt	£4.3.4
	Cash pd Lydia Creekmur per receipt	£7.10
15 Sep	Cash pd James Sikes per receipt	£3.10
18 Sep	Cash pd Amy Dickens per receipt	£5
5 Oct	Cash pd Arthur Curling per receipt	£4.16
13 Oct	Cash pd Thomas Woodward per receipt	£10
	Cash pd William Hall, Jr. per receipt	£4.10
	2 days attendance	18s

	Cash pd Daniel Shirley per order	18s
	Cash pd James Hanbury per order	£1.11.6
	Cash pd for 13 weeks board Julia Shipwash	£4.2.10
	Cash pd James Hanbury for his attending on July Shipwash[13] for 3 weeks	13s 6p
	Cash pd James Grimes, Esquire per order	£23.2.11½
2 Nov	Cash pd Lydia Creekmur per receipt	£3
	Cash pd Nicholas Slack per Col. Joseph Butt order on account of the maintenance of Rebecca Woodward & family	£3
	Cash pd William Hall per receipt	£14
	Cash pd Joseph Harding per order	£4
	Cash pd Joseph Harding on account of Lydia Creekmur	£2.13
	Cash pd Joseph Harding on account of July Shipwash	£6.7.6
	Cash pd Joseph Harding on account of A. Kidd in part of his salary as clerk	£10
	CREDITS	
	Cash rec'd from the collector	£96.3.4
	Cash rec'd from James Boushell being a balance due the parish	£15.2.6

Portsmouth Parish in account with John Pollick Overseer of the Poor

1798	**DEBITS**	
26 Jul	Cash pd Elizabeth Peak per receipt	£2.14
	Cash pd Stephen Anderson per receipt	£5.8
	Cash pd William Carter for keeping Joshua Brown 4½ months	£8.2
	Cash pd Mary Bowers	£2.0.6
	Cash pd James Richardson for 1 week board & nursing Joshua Brown	12s
	Cash pd Joshua Brown funeral expenses	£1.10.6
	Cash pd Maurice Damron	£3.12
13 Aug	Cash pd Margaret Casson	£2.14
17 Sep	Cash pd A. Kidd in favor of John Owens	£7.4
4 Nov	Cash pd Margaret Richardson for keeping Peggy Richardson 3 months	£4.19.0
	4 days attendance	£1.4
	CREDITS	
27 Oct	Cash rec'd from A. Kidd	£13.5.3
	Order on A. Kidd in favor John Owens	£4
30 Oct	Cash rec'd from A. Kidd	4s 6p

[13] July is often used for a more formal Julia.

Portsmouth Parish in account with William Watts Overseer of the Poor

1798	**DEBITS**	
18 Jun	Cash pd Elizabeth House	£10.17.4½
2 Jul	Cash pd Patsey Scott for Harnage's 2 children	£7.6.3
9 Jul	Cash pd Zebe Kellum	£3.2.7½
1 Oct	Cash pd Nelly O'Berry	£3.14.3
31 Jul	Cash pd Thomas Wakefield for William Harris' child	£10.2.1½
22 Aug	Cash pd Elizabeth Wilkins for Thornton's child	£6.14.11½
12 Jul	Cash pd Joseph Carter for self & wife	£5.3.11½
17 Jul	Cash pd Elizabeth Brown	£1.14.7½
27 Sep	Cash pd Mary Combs for self & Britton	£8.7.6
27 Jul	Cash pd Mary Clemmonds	£1.11.6
28 Jul	Cash pd Lankford Godwin per order John Talbot	£3.12
22 Aug	Cash pd John Hardy for keeping John May	£4.10
1 Sep	Cash pd Mathew Howard	£8.7.10½
29 Aug	Cash pd William Britton for keeping John Bunting	£3.11.6
10 Jul	Cash pd William Plummer for Peggy Richardson	9s ½p
	Order on Mr. Kidd in favor of William Plummer	£2.12.½
	4 days attendance (self)	£1.4
16 Oct	Cash pd Lydia Manson	£1.19.4½
17 Oct	Cash pd Mary Combs Britton	10s 6p
23 Oct	Cash pd William Britton for keeping John Bunting	£3.0.2
27 Oct	Cash pd William Britton for keeping John Bunting	£8.2
	Cash pd Daniel Hall for making Joseph Britton's coffin	18s
	Cash pd Daniel Hall for making his funeral service	12s
	Cash pd Mathew Howard	£1.4
31 Oct	Cash pd William Britton for keeping John Bunting	10s 4½p
	Cash pd Mary Combs Britton	£1.11.6
	Cash pd Elizabeth Wilkins for Thornton's child	18s
	Order on Mr. Kidd in favor of Mr. Cotton	£1.10
	Cash pd Mary Combs Britton	10s 6p
	Cash pd for digging Britton's grave	4s 6p
	1 day attendance	6s
	CREDITS	
	Cash rec'd of Andrew Kidd, collector	£10.10
	Cash rec'd of Andrew Kidd, collector	£12
	Cash rec'd of Andrew Kidd, collector	£13.4
	Cash rec'd of Andrew Kidd, collector	£3.1.6
	Cash rec'd from Capt. Oldner for his bond	£6
	Cash rec'd for Andrew Kidd, collector	£6
	Cash rec'd at our meeting	£4
17 Oct	Cash rec'd of Dr. O'Grady in part his bond	£8.2
26 Oct	Cash rec'd of Andrew Kidd, collector	£15.18
	Order in favor Mr. Cotton	£1.10

Elizabeth River Parish in account with John Holland Overseer of the Poor

1798	**DEBITS**	
16 Aug	Cash pd to George Townsend	£1.1
4 Sep	Cash pd to James Cooper	£3.6
9 Oct	Cash pd to James Cooper	£1.13
13 Oct	Cash pd to Mrs. Wilder	£2
15 Oct	Cash pd to Mrs. Wilder	£2
	Cash pd for articles furnished Mr. Angel & his family in the smallpox by order Overseers of the Poor	£7.18.3
18 Jun	4 days attendance annual meeting at Ferry Point at Mr. Herbert's	£1.4
	Cash pd the amount of Joshua Oldner account for boarding and nursing 9 Parish Negroes when under inoculation for the smallpox	£10.3.7
	Cash pd on Mr. A. Kidd, collector, in favor of James Cooper for keeping Dinah Cooper	£1.10
Oct	2 days attendance	12s
	Cash pd to Mrs. Millison	£1.16.3
	Cash pd to Francis Millison	£4
	To the collection of £83	£4.19.7
	Cash pd to Ed Valentine (Ann Townsend order)	£3.12
	Cash pd to George Townsend	£3
	Cash pd to Francis Wilder	£10.0.6
	Cash pd to James Cooper	£8
	Cash pd to Mrs. Angel	£8.18
	7 days hiring out the Parish Negroes	£2.2
	Cash pd to Foster for crying Parish Negroes & bonds	£2.2
	Cash pd to James, Dinah & John Cooper	£6
	CREDITS	
6 Aug	Cash rec'd of Mrs. Street's bond for hire a Negro girl	£5.10
	Cash rec'd of Dr. O'Grady in part his bond	£6
	Order on Mr. A. Kidd, collector, in favor of James Cooper for keeping Dinah Cooper	£1.10
	Cash rec'd of Dr. O'Grady his bond	£12
	Cash rec'd of Henry Durant's his bond	£7.12.3
	Cash rec'd of Dr. O'Grady in part his bond	£9
	Cash rec'd of G. Robinson in part	£18.12
	Cash rec'd of Abner Cox (a note)	£3
	Cash rec'd of James Douglas (bond)	£5
	Cash rec'd in part A. Campbell's note	£3.3
	Cash rec'd Penelope 2 quarters hire	£1.16
	Cash rec'd for hire of Peg	£1.4
	Cash rec'd for hire of Mary	6s
	Cash rec'd of William Watts	£18
	Cash rec'd of Henry Durant's bond	£5.1.6

At a Court held for Norfolk County the 22nd day of May 1798

William Godfrey and William Colley having been elected Overseers of the Poor in the Parish of Elizabeth River and summoned to appear here and qualify, but failing to do so, Gersham Nimmo & John Holland are by the court appointed Overseers of the Poor in their stead. Ordered that they be summoned to appear at the next court and qualify to their appointment.

A copy teste: William Wilson

Sir, Please for to let my son have a little money for me as I am in great want of some and you'd greatly oblige your humble servant.

[signed] Sarah Eastwood 5 Nov 1798 For Mr. James Brown

Rec'd this 8 Nov 1798 of James Brown, Overseer of the Poor, the sum of $2 dollars for Sarah Eastwood, parishioner.

[signed] Jesse *(his mark)* Eastwood

Rec'd this 8th day of Nov 1798 of James Brown, Overseer of the Poor, the sum of 13s 6p as part payment for keeping Ann Isdel & child up to 26 Sep 1798

Ann *(her mark)* Harris

Rec'd this 27th day of Nov 1798 of James Brown, Overseer of the Poor, the sum of $2 for Ann Harris in part for keeping Ann Isdel and one child up to 26 Sep 1798

John *(his mark)* Carney

4 Sep 1798 Rec'd of James Brown, Overseer of the Poor, the sum of £3.9.8 in full of the balance due on John Taboot's [Talbot's] books (late Overseer of the Poor) for keeping Lavina Ross.

Henry *(his mark)* Pulling

9 Jul 1798 Rec'd of William Watts, Overseer of the Poor, the sum of £3 in part of the money due me from the parish.

Nelly *(her mark)* O'Berry Teste: Sam Smith

1 Oct 1798 Rec'd of William Watts, Overseer of the Poor, the sum of 6s 9p in part of the money due me from the parish

Nelly *(her mark)* O'Berry Teste: Sam Smith

13 Oct [1798] Rec'd of William Watts, Overseer of the Poor, of the sum of 7s 6p in part of the money due me from the parish.

Nelly *(her mark)* O'Berry Teste: Sam Smith

2 Jul 1798 Received of William Watts, Overseer of the Poor, the sum of £7.2.6 in part of the money due me from the parish for keeping John and Peggy Harnage.

Patsey *(her mark)* Scott Teste: Samuel Walker

6 Sep *[1798]* Received of William Watts the sum of 3s 9p in part of the money due me for keeping Peggy Harnage.

Patsey *(her mark)* Scott Teste: Samuel Walker

9 Jul 1798 Received of William Watts, Overseer of the Poor, the sum of £3 in part of the money due me from the parish.
Nelly *(her mark)* O'Berry Teste: Sam Smith

1 Oct 1798 Received of William Watts, Overseer of the Poor, the sum of 6s 9p in part of the money due me from the parish.
Nelly *(her mark)* O'Berry Teste: Sam Smith

13 Oct 1798 Received of William Watts, Overseer of the Poor, the sum of 7s 6p in part of the money due me from the parish.
Nelly *(her mark)* O'Berry Teste: Sam Cutherell

22 Aug 1798 Received of William Watts, Overseer of the Poor, the sum of £7.5.4 money in part of the money due me from the parish.
Mathew *(his mark)* Howard Teste: Peter Harford

1 Sep 1798 Received of William Watts, Overseer of the Poor, the sum of 16s 6p in part of the money due me from this parish.
Mathew *(his mark)* Howard Teste: John Pollick

17 Jul 1798 Received of William Watts, Overseer of the Poor, the sum of £1.14.7 money in part of the money due me from this parish.
Elizabeth *(her mark)* Brown Teste: James Gaskins

Mr. John Hardy claim for keeping John May as allowed in March last amounts to 4 pounds 10s.
[signed] Andrew Kidd The Overseers of Portsmouth Parish 20 Aug 1798

29 Jun 1798 Received of William Watts, Overseer of the Poor, the sum of £10.11.4 money in part of the money due me from the parish.
Elizabeth Hoacey Teste: James Gaskins

20 Sep *[1798]* Received of William Watts, Overseer of the Poor, the sum of 6s in part of the money due me from the parish
Elizabeth Hoacey Teste: Joshua Haynes

20 Sep *[1798]* Received of William Watts, Overseer of the Poor, the sum of £1.0.3 in part of the money due me for keeping Thornton's child.
Elizabeth *(her mark)* Wilkins Teste: Samuel Cutherell

4 Oct *[1798]* Received of William Watts, Overseer of the Poor, the sum of $2 in part of the money due me from the Parish.
Elizabeth *(her mark)* Wilkins Teste: Samuel Cutherell

9 Oct 1798 Received of William Watts, Overseer of the Poor, the sum of 18s in part of the money due me for keeping the Thornton child.
Elizabeth *(her mark)* Wilkins Teste: Wm Porter

12 Jul 1798 Received of William Watts, Overseer of the Poor, the sum of £4.2.2 in part of the money due me and my wife from the parish.
Joseph *(his mark)* Carter Teste: James Buxton

7 Sep 1798 Received of William Watts, Overseer of the Poor, the sum of 9s 9p in part of the money due me and my wife from the parish.
Joseph *(his mark)* Carter Teste: Samuel Walker

23 Oct 1798 Received of William Watts, Overseer of the Poor, the sum of £3.0.2 in part of the money due me for keeping John Buntin
William *(his mark)* Britton Teste: Frances Dayes

27 Oct 1798 Received of William Watts, Overseer of the Poor, the sum of £8.0.2 in part of the money due me for keeping John Buntin.
William *(his mark)* Britton Teste: Samuel Cutherell

1 Nov 1798 Received of William Watts, Overseer of the Poor, the sum of 10s 1p in part of the money due me for keeping John Buntin.
William *(his mark)* Britton Teste: William Veale

10 Jul 1798 Paid William Plummer for Peggy Richardson 9s and half penny for an order on Mr. Kidd in favor of Mrs. Plummer for Fanny Peake[14] the sum of £2.12 half pence.

Elizabeth River Parish to John Holland

1798	**DEBITS**	
16 Aug	Cash pd to Mr. Gregory Townson	*[torn]*
4 Sep	Cash pd to Mr. James Cooper	£3.6
9 Oct	Cash pd to Mr. James Cooper	£1.13
13 Oct	Cash pd to Mrs. Wilder	£2
15 Oct	Cash pd to Miss Wilder	£2
	Cash & articles furnished Mr. Angel and his family in the small pox, by orders of the Overseers of the Poor	£7.18.3
18 Jun	4 days attendance at annual meetings at Mr. Herbert's at Ferry Point	£1.4
	Cash pd *[creased and worn]* orders account for nursing and boarding 9 parish Negroes when under inoculation for the small pox	£10.3.7
	Order on Mr. A. Kidd, collector, in favor Mr. James Cooper for keeping Dinah Cooper	£1.10
Oct	2 days attendance	12s

14 As an example of the inconsistencies, this entry is in the ledger portion but Fanny is not mentioned.

1799		
19 Sep	Cash pd to Miss Millison	£1.16.3
7 Aug	Cash pd Francis Millison	£4
	Amount of sundrys	£113.13.9
	Sum paid Edward Valentine per order George Townsend	£3.12
1798	**CREDITS**	
16 Aug	Cash rec'd of Mrs. Street's bond	8s
30 Aug	Cash rec'd of D. O'Grady bond	£6
	Order on A. Kidd, collector, in favor of James Cooper for D. Cooper	£1.10
	Cash rec'd of D. O'Grady bond	£12
	Cash rec'd by H. Durant's bond	£7.12.3
	Cash rec'd balance of Miss Street's bond	£5
1799	Cash rec'd part of D. O'Grady's bond	£9
	Cash rec'd of G. Robinson's bond	£12.12
	Cash rec'd of James Douglas' bond	£5
	Cash rec'd of A. Campbell part of note	£3.3
	Cash rec'd of Penelope for her 2 quarters hire	£1.16
	Cash rec'd for the hire of one Negro Pegg	£1.4
	Cash rec'd for the hire of one Negro Mary	6s

27 Oct 1798 Received of William Watts, Overseer of the Poor, the sum of 18s for making a coffin for Joseph Britton
Samuel Hall Teste: L. Buxton

List of Names with numbers[15]
John Lee 1
Malachi Maund 2
Dickerson Prior 3
Samuel Bacon 4
Josiah Truss 5
Bennet Armstrong 6
William Stevenson 7
Samuel Tomlinson 8
Richard Bickerdick 9
William Skinkar 10
Thomas Morris 11
George Wilson 12

11 July 1798 Received of William Watts, Overseer of the Poor, the sum of £4.7.2 in part of the money due me from parish for keeping Nelson Thornton and myself.
Elizabeth *(her mark)* Wilkins Teste: Ann Jefferson

[15] This is a list of names with numbers 1 through 12 as if they were listing a possible jury, date unknown. It's included here as it was in the papers at the archives.

22 Aug 1798 Received of William Watts, Overseer of the Poor, the sum of 15s 6p in part of the money due me for Nelson Worington[16] and myself from the parish.
Elizabeth *(her mark)* Wilkins Teste Robert Peed

16 Oct 1798 Received of William Watts, Overseer of the Poor, the sum £1.19.4 in part of the money due me from the parish.
Lydia *(her mark)* Manson Teste: Elizabeth Manson

31 Jul 1798 Received of William Watts, Overseer of the Poor, the sum of £6.18.9 in part of the money due me from the parish for keeping Thomas Hare's child
Ann *(her mark)* Wakefield Teste: Robert Peed

5 Sep 1798 Received of William Watts, Overseer of the Poor, the sum of £3.0.4 for Thomas Hare's child on the parish
Thomas *(his mark)* Wakefield Teste: Samuel Cutherell

9 Jul 1798 Received of William Watts, Overseer of the Poor, the sum of £2.14 in part of the money due me from the parish
Gebedy *(his mark)* Kellum Teste: Ann Jefferson

8 Oct 1798 Received of William Watts, Overseer of the Poor, the sum of 8s 7p in part of the money due me from the parish.
Gebedy *(his mark)* Kellum Teste: Robert Peed

22 Aug 1798 Received of William Watts, Overseer of the Poor, the sum of £4.10 for keeping John May agreeable to an order by the Overseers in March.
John Hardy Teste: Samuel Walker

28 Jul 1798 Received of William Watts, Overseer of the Poor, the sum of £3.12 in full of an order from Mr. Talbot
Lankford Godwin Teste: Samuel Cutherell

27 *[torn]* 1798 Received of William Watts, Overseer of the Poor, the sum of £1.11.6 in part of the money due me from the parish.
Mary *(her mark)* Clemons Teste: Samuel Walker

28 Oct 1798 Received of William Watts, Overseer of the Poor, the sum of 12s in part of the money due Joseph Britton.
Mary *(her mark)* Combs Britton Teste: Francis Graham

17 Sep 1798 Received the sum of 10s 6p in part of the money due me from the parish.
Mary *(her mark)* Combs Britton Teste: Samuel Cutherell

31 Oct 1798 Received of William Watts, Overseer of the Poor, the sum of £1.11.6 in part of the money due me in part from the parish.
Mary *(her mark)* Combs Britton Teste: *[illegible]*

---

[16] It's possible this should be Nelson Thornton as above, but it is definitely written as Worington.

14 Nov 1798 Received of William Watts, Overseer of the Poor, the sum of 10s 6p in part of the money due me from the parish.
Mary *(her mark)* Combs Britton Teste: *[folded]*

22 Sep 1798 Received of William Watts, Overseer of the Poor, the sum of 18s in part of the money due me and Joseph Britton.
Mary *(her mark)* Combs Britton Teste: Michael Bard

27 Sep 1798 Received of William Watts, Overseer of the Poor, the sum of 7s in part of the money due me and Joseph Britton.
Mary *(her mark)* Combs Britton Teste: Daniel Hall

14 Aug 1798 Received of William Watts, Overseer of the Poor, the sum of £6 in part of the money due me and Joseph Britton from the parish.
Mary *(her mark)* Combs Britton Teste: Samuel Walker

1 Sep 1798 Rec'd of William Watts, Overseer of the Poor, the sum of 10s 6p in part of the money due me and Joseph Britton.
Mary *(her mark)* Combs Britton Teste: Solomon Hodges

29 Aug 1798 Received of William Watts, Overseer of the Poor, of the sum of £1.15.1 in part of the money due me for keeping Bunton as a parishioner.
William *(his mark)* Britton Teste: Solomon Hodges

27 Sep 1798 Received of William Watts, Overseer of the Poor, the sum of £1.16.4 in part of the money due me for keeping John Bunton as a parishioner.
William *(his mark)* Britton Teste: Hartford *[rest missing]*

22 Sep 1798 Received of William Watts, Overseer of the Poor, the sum of 2 dollars in part of the money due me and my wife from the Parish.
Joseph *(his mark)* Carter Teste: James Gaskins

19 Feb 1799 Received of William Watts, Overseer of Poor, the sum of £1.14.7 in part of the money due me and my wife from the parish.
Joseph *(his mark)* Carter Teste: Solomon Hodges

12 Oct 1798 Received of William Watts, Overseer of the Poor, the sum of 6s in part of the money due me from the parish.
Mathew *(his mark)* HowardTeste: Samuel Cutherell

30 Oct 1798 Received of William Watts, Overseer of Poor, the sum of £1.4 in part of the money due Mathew Howard from the parish.
Fanny Howard Teste: Francis Peed

19 Jan 1799 Received of William Watts, Overseer of the Poor, the sum of £1.3.9 in part of the money due me from the parish.
Lydia *(her mark)* Manson Teste S. Toomer

William Watts for the Parish of Norfolk County to Samuel Hall
15 Oct 1798 Making Coffin Joseph Britton 18s
Rec'd payment from the above Samuel Hall

9 Apr 1799 Received of William Watts, Overseer of the Poor, the sum of 15s 9p in full Sep to 2 Mar 1799
Mathew *(his mark)* Howard Teste Samuel Cutherell

10 Apr 1799 Received of William Watts, Overseer of the Poor, the sum of £5.18.6 in full of my account from Sep to 27 Apr 1799
Elizabeth House Teste Samuel Cutherell

10 Apr 1799 Received of William Watts, Overseer of the Poor, the sum of £2.2 by orders of the Overseer of the Poor
Caty *(her mark)* Owens Teste: Ann Jefferson

1 Mar 1799 Rec'd of William Watts, Overseer of the Poor, the sum of £6.13.9 due me from the parish.
Mathew *(his mark)* HowardTeste: Solomon Hodges

1 Mar 1799 Rec'd of William Watts, Overseer of the Poor, the sum of £1.4.9 in part of the money due me from the parish.
Lydy *(her mark)* Manson Teste: James Matthews

1 Mar 1799 Rec'd of William Watts, Overseer of the Poor, the sum of 16s 6p due me from the parish.
Mary *(her mark)* Clemmonds Teste: Richard Barr

1 Mar 1799 Rec'd of William Watts, Overseer of the Poor, the sum of *[torn]* pounds 7s and 7p part of the money due me from the parish.
Mary *(her mark)* Com*[torn]* Teste: D. Watson

1 Mar 1799 Rec'd of William Watts, Overseer of the Poor, the sum of *[torn]* pounds 11s in part of the money due me from the parish.
Eliza *(her mark)* W*[torn]* Teste: Richard Kesick

1799 - 1800 Entries

8 Apr 1799 Received of William Watts, Overseer of the Poor, the sum of £2.11.6 in full for Thornton's child and myself to the 1 Feb 1799
Elizabeth *(her mark)* Wilkins Teste: James Gaskins

8 Apr 1799 Received of William Watts, Overseer of the Poor, the sum of £2.6.10 in full up to Feb 1, 1799
[illegible] (her mark) Kellum Teste: Ann Jefferson

8 Apr 1799 Received of William Watts, Overseer of the Poor, the sum of £1.16 in full up to 1 Feb 1799
Mary *(her mark)* Clemmons Teste: R. Peed

9 Apr 1799 Received of William Watts, Overseer of the Poor, the sum of $2 by orders of the Overseers of the Poor at our last meeting

Ann *(her mark)* Eagles Teste: S. Toomer

Portsmouth Parish in account with William Watts Overseer of the Poor

1799	DEBITS	
	Cash pd Elizabeth House 3 children	£16.13.1½
	Cash pd Patsey Scott for keeping John & Peggy Harnage	£4
	Cash pd Libby Kellum	7.16½
	Cash pd Nelly O'Berry	7.16½
	Cash pd Thomas Wakefield for Willis Eastwood's child	£1.15.4½
	Cash pd Ann Hazel in time of sickness	12s
	Cash pd Elizabeth Wilkins and Nelson Thornton	£17.16.2½
	Cash pd Joseph Carter and wife	£19.10
	Cash pd Dr. Leigh	£18
	Cash pd Elizabeth Brown	£4.4
	3 days attendance at meeting	18s
	Cash pd hiring out Negroes	6s
	Cash pd Ann Fitzgerald keeping John Culpeper	£4.5.9
	Cash pd Mary McLenan	£1.16
	Cash pd Magnien by order the meeting	£1.10
	Cash pd clothes advance Will Snale	£2.1.4½
	Cash pd John Holland	£18
	Cash pd Mary Garnes in distress	12s
	Cash pd Joseph & Mary Britton	£11.12.11½
	Cash pd Mary Clemmonds	£3.4
	Cash pd Mathew Howard	£20.10.9
	Cash pd Mathew Owens in distress	£2.2
	Cash pd Lydia Mason	£1.4.9
	Cash pd William Britton for keeping John Bunting	£20.6.6
	Cash pd Caty Owens	£6.18
	Cash pd Mary Combs	£1.1
	Cash pd Elizabeth Wilkins	£1.16
	Cash pd Mary Combs	£1.1
	Cash pd Nelly O'Berry	11s 3p
	Cash pd Mary Combs	£1.1
	Cash pd Elizabeth House	15s
1799	**CREDITS**	
	Cash rec'd from Andrew Kidd, collector	£121
	Cash rec'd from treasurer Norfolk County per order court	£90
	Cash rec'd from Dr. O'Grady	£9.18
	Cash rec'd from James Brown for Will Snale's hire	£3.17.6

St. Brides Parish in account with Jordan Marchant Overseer of the Poor

1798	**DEBITS**	
2 Dec	Cash pd Mary Creekmur per receipt	£4.10
1799		
2 Jan	Cash pd Mathew Butler per receipt	18s
	Cash pd Danger per receipt	£4.16
	Cash pd Thomas Messer per receipt	£4.16
5 Jan	Cash pd Arthur Curling per receipt	£3.12
2 Feb	Cash pd Francis Boush per receipt	£4.10.10
	Cash pd Lydia Creekmur per receipt	£4.10
15 Feb	Cash pd James Sikes and son per receipt	£6.15
2 Mar	Cash pd Daniel Shirley per receipt	£1.16
	Cash pd Mary Creekmur per receipt	£3.7.6
16 Mar	Cash pd Amy Dickens per receipt	£3.15
2 Apr	Cash pd Thomas Messer per receipt	£3.12
	Cash pd Lydia Creekmur per receipt	£1.10
2 Jul	Cash pd Mary Creekmur per receipt	£4.10
	Cash pd James Sikes & son per receipt	£8.15
	Cash pd James Hall per receipt	18s
	Cash pd Edward Jones per receipt	£3.1
31 Jul	Cash pd William Creekmur per receipt	4s 6p
	Cash pd Thomas Messer per receipt	£7.10
	Cash pd Lydia Creekmur per receipt	£4.16
	Cash pd William Griggs per receipt	£4.16
	Cash pd Caleb Wilson per receipt	£1.10
	Cash pd Timothy Wood per receipt	£6.10
	Cash pd Timothy Wood per receipt	£3.5
	Cash pd Stephen Sikes per receipt	£3
	Cash pd John Shepherd per receipt	£3.5.10
	Cash pd Arthur Curling 5 months up to his death	£7.10
	Cash pd Mason Shipwash	£3.14.10
2 Sep	1 day attendance	6s
	Cash pd Judith Deal	11s 7½p
	Cash pd Thomas Messer per receipt	£7.10
	Cash pd Zach Douge per receipt	£9.12
	Cash pd James Hanbury per receipt	£6
Oct	Cash pd Timothy Wood per receipt	£1.19
	Cash pd Amy Dickens	£4.7.6
	Cash pd Susannah Bell	£4.10
	Cash pd clerk's tickets	11s 4½p
	Cash pd Lydia Sivels for keeping orphan	£2
	Cash pd Abiah Creekmur per receipt	£4.10
	Cash pd Penelope Manning per receipt	£9.12
	Cash pd Susannah Bell	£1.16
	Cash pd Thomas Messer	£6
	Cash pd Col. Butt his balance	£25.13.4½
	Cash pd Mary Creekmur per receipt	£3.7.6
	Cash pd James Manning for Lydia Creekmur	£8.8

	Cash pd Dr. Harding for his year salary	£18
	Cash pd Penelope Manning	£4.16
	Cash pd James Hanbury	£7.4.6
	Cash pd Thomas Messer	£6
	Cash pd James Hanbury	£2
	Cash pd Amy Dickens	£3.15
	Cash pd Timothy Wood	£4.11
	Cash pd Ann Manning on account Pen. Manning	£4.16
	Cash pd Ann Manning on account Pen. Manning	£4
	Balance Thomas Messer 1 month	£1.9.6½
	Cash pd Simon Jackson on account Thomas Messer funeral and expenses	£3.6.1
	Cash pd Timothy Wood per receipt	£1.6
	Cash pd Samuel Wiles on account Amy Dickens	£2.14
	Cash pd Dr. Blamire in full of Wilkins note	£10.18
	Cash pd William Warden's account	£6.18
	Cash pd Susannah Banks 3 months & 2 children	£3.16.9
	Cash pd William Griggs per receipt	£2.8
	Cash pd Dr. Harding 19 days William Warden	£2.11
	Cash pd James Wilkins per receipt	£2.13.5
	Cash pd Abiah Creekmur per receipt	£3.7.6
	Cash pd James Manning per receipt	£4.16
	Cash pd Abiah Creekmur per receipt	£3.7.6
	Cash pd Zach Douge per receipt	£4.10
	Cash pd for coffin, digging grave, finding shirt, sheet, etc. for Adam Creamer	£1.10
1800		
	Cash pd James Sikes per receipt	£24.10
	Cash pd Penelope Manning per receipt	£2.14
	Cash pd Edward Creekmur per receipt	£6.15
	Cash pd Malachi Corbell per receipt	£6
	Cash pd William Gwyn per receipt	£12.14.7½
	Cash pd Benjamin Millar Hill per receipt	£1.10
	Cash pd Mary Baxter per receipt	£8.5
	Cash pd Timothy Wood per receipt	£5.4
	Cash pd John Armstrong, Jr. on account Benjamin Dukes	£21.19.10½
	Cash pd James Manning	£9.12
	Cash pd George Hall poor tax	16s 6p
	Cash pd Zach Douge	£6.6
	Cash pd Mary Baxter	£6.12
	Cash pd William Griggs	£9.12
	Cash pd Samuel Stafford for William Griggs coffin	18s
	Cash pd James Hanbury	£4
	Cash pd James Hanbury	£7
	Cash pd on account Benjamin Dukes	£5.17
	Cash pd on account an orphan child	£2.18.1½
	Cash pd William Griggs 2¾ months	£3.6

	Cash pd Adam Randolph for moving one of the poor out of the county	12s
	Cash pd Benjamin Dukes per receipt	£5.18.5
	Cash pd Mary Creekmur per receipt	£7.17.6
	Cash pd Malachi Corbell per receipt	£6.4.6
	Cash pd Mary Baxter per receipt	15s
	Cash pd Tled *[?]* Hays on account Cartwright	£3.15
	Cash pd Dinah Stewart account Lydia Creekmur	£1.4
	Cash pd Jeremiah Butt on account Thomas Burfoot	£2.17.9
	Cash pd Mary Suggs on account Jonah Suggs	18s
	Cash pd Andrew Banks on account S. Read	£25.4
	Cash pd Malachi Corbell per receipt	£1.10
	Cash pd Keziah Huliot *[?]* per receipt	£7.10
	Cash pd Dr. Harding per receipt	£18
	Cash pd Andrew Kidd per receipt	£6.19.6
10 Mar	Cash pd Amy Dickens	£7.4
15 Sep	Cash pd James Sikes	£12.5
	Cash pd John Boushell	9s
	CREDITS	
1798	Cash rec'd Richard Webb, balance of his collections	£45.58
1799	Cash rec'd John Butt, collector	£134.10.7
1800	Cash rec'd John Butt, collector	£261
1801	Cash rec'd Alexander Grimes in part his collection this year	£150

Elizabeth River Parish in account with John Holland Overseer of the Poor

1798	**DEBITS**	
	Durant's bond paid Edward Valentine	£5.1.6
	Gilbert Robinson bond paid James Cooper	£18.12
	Cash pd James Cooper	£2.2
	Cash pd William Peaton	£7.10
	Cash pd George Townsend	£1.4
	Cash pd Mrs. Angel	£8.1.3
	Cash pd Mrs. Millison	£3
	Cash pd William Peaton	£5
	Cash pd Dr. O'Grady	£1.2.6
	Cash pd Joshua Peaton	£7
	Cash pd for a coffin & funeral, one of the poor	£1.13
	Cash pd William Peaton for burying one of the poor	£1.19.9
1799		
	1 day attendance & ferriage	6s 9p
	Cash pd William Stacks	18s
22 Nov	Cash pd Frances Millison for keeping children	£2
6 Dec	Cash pd Elizabeth Townsend	£1.4
21 Dec	Cash pd Joshua Peaton	£2.2

1800		
6 Jan	Cash pd William Bird	£3
7 Jan	8 days hiring out the Parish Negroes	0.0.0
	Cash pd William Peaton for orphans	£5.18
	Cash pd Isaac Anderson for coffin	18s
8 Jan	Cash pd Mr. Foster for bonds & services	15s
9 Jan	Cash pd John Hutcheson for taking up Negroes	3s
10 Jan	Cash pd John Wilkins per order overseer	3s
11 Jan	Cash pd Winifred Angel	£8.2
14 Jan	Cash pd Frances Millison for her children	£2
	Cash pd Edward Colony for making coffin in Dec	18s
Feb	Board of Edward Dewier 1 month	£1.4
10 Mar	Cash pd jacket and trousers 7/6 shirt 3/9	£1.1.6
	Cash pd Frances Millison for her children	£1
11 Mar	Cash pd Jos. Bartlet for burial a dead man	£2.2
2 Apr	Cash pd William Peaton for orphans	£5.18
	Cash pd William Peaton for orphans 7 Jan (omitted)	£3
10 Apr	Cash pd Thomas Lambert for Nancy Dunton	£3.15

Norfolk County in account current with John Butt Collector of the Poor Tax for St. Brides

1799	**DEBITS**	
	Cash pd Jordan Marchant, Overseer of the Poor, at different times	£134.10.7
	Cash pd William Bartee orders in favor sundry people	£67.15.8
	Cash pd Jordan Marchant	£22.4.9
	Insolvents	£3.12
	Commission at 10%	£25.7
1799	**CREDITS**	
	Collection of 1,690 tithables being the number taken per list for St. Brides Parish for the year 1799	£253.10

12 Jun 1799 Received of William Watts, Overseer of the Poor, the sum of £3.7 for bonding John Culpeper, for child in the parish.

Nancy *(her mark)* Peck *[?]* Jenett Teste: Sally Cron

3 days attendance at our meeting of the Overseers 18s
1 day attendance at the hiring out of the Parish Negroes 6s

14 June 1799 Received of William Watts, Overseer of the Poor, the sum of 17s 9p Sep to 1 May 1799

Gelidy *(his mark)* Kellum Teste: Ann Jefferson

14 Jun 1799 Received of William Watts, Overseer of the Poor, the sum of 40s for 2 months up to the 24 Jun 1799

Mary *(her mark)* Combs Teste: Solomon Hodges

[torn] 1799 Received of William Watts, Overseer of the Poor, the sum of $2 agreeable to the orders of the overseers
Caty *(her mark)* Owens Teste: S. Toomer

10 Jun 1799 Received of William Watts, Overseer of the Poor, the sum of £1.7 for Nelson Thornton and myself to 1 May 1799.
Elizabeth *(her mark)* Wilkins Teste: Samuel Cutherell

11 Jun 1799 Received of William Watts, Overseer of the Poor, the sum of $5 as cash due me from the Parish.
Nelly *(her mark)* O'Berry Teste: James Gaskins

11 Jun 1799 Received of William Watts, Overseer of the Poor, the sum of $2 agreeable an order of the Overseers of the Poor
Caty *(her mark)* Owens Teste: Richard Kelsick

31 Jan 1799 Received of James Brown, Overseer of the Poor, the sum of 13s to buy a pair of shoes and some clothing for me.
Sarah *(her mark)* Perkins

Rec'd this 24 Jan 1799 of James Brown, Overseer of the Poor, the sum of $8 dollars being in part of Sarah Eastwood yearly allowance for Sarah Eastwood.
Jesse *(his mark)* Eastwood

5 Feb 1799 Rec'd of James Brown, Overseer of the Poor, the sum of 18s in full of the balance due on John Talbot's books for keeping Martha Powell one month also 7s in part for keeping John Spring this present year.
Margaret *(her mark)* Tucker Teste: Thomas Lancaster

23 Feb 1799 Rec'd of James Brown, Overseer of the Poor, the sum of £4.8.1.half penny in part for Sarah Perkins allowance while with me.
Thomas Archer Teste: Stephen Bell

25 Mar 1799 Rec'd of James Brown, Overseer of the Poor, the sum of £2.7.7 half penny for Cloe Taylor parishioner
Thomas *(his mark)* Powell

1 Apr 1799 Burying Mrs. Colony one of the poor of the parish 12s
Alexander McDaniel

18 Apr 1799 Rec'd of Gersham Nimmo the sum of 13s 6p being my full allowance for 1 month commencing 26 Feb and ending 26 Mar 1799 agreeable to order of the meeting.
Elizabeth *(her mark)* Riddle Teste: Richard Lee

18 Jun 1799 Rec'd of Gersham Nimmo 4 pounds of sugar, 3 pecks of meal and 3s 6p in cash it being my full allowance from 10 May up to 10 Jun 1799, in full
James *(his mark)* Guy Witness: William Walker

Rec'd 11 Jul 1799 from Gersham Nimmo the sum of £2.4.4 being my parish requisition for keeping children.
Louisa *(her mark)* Archer   Teste: Thomas Lee

8 Feb 1799 Rec'd of James Brown, Overseer of the Poor, the sum of £6.17 in part for keeping Margaret Powell the year 1798
Lemuel Powell

Sir,
Please pay Miss Keziah Cooper 4 pounds 10s for one quarter's board of Frances Chapman from 1 Mar last to 1 Jun. I believe there is more than a year's board independent of this still due her father's estate for the board of Frances Chapman but she is in a good deal of distress and unable to board Frances Chapman without the moneys being paid as it comes due. I think it would be as well pay her before the estate is paid in *[folded area]* however as you may think just.
S.B. Talbot
14 Jul 1799

[reverse] Received of Gersham Nimmo the within sum of £4.10 as it being for the board of Frances Chapman from 1 Mar up to 1 Jun 1799
Keziah Cooper   Teste: Hillery (his mark) Williams

18 Oct 1799 Rec'd from James Brown, Overseer of the Poor, the sum of $10 dollars being in full for keeping Lavina Ross, parishioner, up to 26 Sep 1799
Henry *(his mark)* Pulling

8 Oct 1799 Received of James Brown, Overseer of the Poor, the sum of £2.3 being part for keeping Ivy's orphans up to 28 Sep last for Mary Bowers
Thomas Lancaster

6 Sep 1799 Rec'd of James Brown, Overseer of the Poor, the sum of 1 dollar, being to buy some clothing
Sarah *(her mark)* Perkins

28 Sep 1799 Rec'd of James Brown, Overseer of the Poor, the sum of £2.5 being in full for keeping Richard Rose up to 2 Sep the present year
John *(his mark)* Rose

16 Oct 1799 Rec'd of Gersham Nimmo 5 pounds and half of pork, a half bushel of meal, three pounds of sugar, 1 pound of coffee, the whole amounting 12. It being my full allowance up to 10 Oct 1799
James *(his mark)* Guy   Teste: William Walker

21 Dec 1798 Rec'd of James Brown, Overseer of the Poor, the sum of £1.2 in part for keeping Smith Stafford
Elizabeth *(her mark)* Stafford

5 Feb 1799 Rec'd of James Brown, Overseer of the Poor, the sum of £7.59 in part for keeping two orphan children the years 1797-1798 for Mary Bowers
Thomas Lancaster

18 Oct 1799 Rec'd from James Brown, Overseer of the Poor, the sum of $3.50 in part for keeping John Spring parishioner for the year 1799
Henry Pulling

10 Apr 1799 Rec'd of Gersham Nimmo the sum of $10 dollars in part for keeping a poor boy, Henry Davis, for the year 1798.
James Davis Teste: Thomas Lee

28 May 1799 Rec'd of Gersham Nimmo a bond of Richard Bailey amounting to 26 *[dollars?]* to collect it being delivered to me for my services in part to the poor of Elizabeth River Parish.
W. Starke

16 Oct 1799 Rec'd of Gersham Nimmo the sum of £4.10 it being the sum allowed for keeping Frances Chapman from 1 Jun to 1 Sep
Keziah Cooper

Rec'd 1 Mar 1799 of William Watts, Overseer of the Poor, the sum of £6.5.9 in part of the money due me from the parish.
Elizabeth House Teste: Solomon Hodges

1 Mar 1799 William Watts, Overseer of the Poor, the sum of £3.14 in part of the money due me for keeping John and Peggy Harnage
Patsey *(her mark)* Scott Teste: R. Peed

1 Mar 1799 William Watts, Overseer of the Poor, the sum of £1.12 in part of the money due me from the parish.
Zibbie *(her mark)* Kellum Teste: Ann Jefferson

1 Mar 1799 William Watts, Overseer of the Poor, the sum of £5.17.1 in part of the money due me from the parish.
Nelly *(her mark)* O'Berry Teste: Samuel Walker

1 Mar 1799 William Watts, Overseer of the Poor, the sum of £9.6.6 for John Buntin one of the parishioners
William *(his mark)* Britton Teste: Samuel Cutherell

1 Mar 1799 William Watts Overseer of the Poor the sum of £6.13.9 in part of the money due me from parish.
Mathew *(his mark)* Howard Teste: Solomon Hodges

1 Mar 1799 William Watts Overseer of the Poor the sum of £1.4.9 in part of the money due me from Parish.
Lydy *(her mark)* Manson Teste: James Mathews

1 Mar 1799 William Watts Overseer of the Poor the sum of 6s 6p in part of the money due me from Parish.
Mary *(her mark)* Clemmonds Teste: Richard Barr

1 Mar 1799 William Watts Overseer of the Poor the sum of *[fold]* pound 7s and 7p in part of the money due me from Parish.

Mary *(her mark)* Combs Teste: D. Watts

1 Mar 1799 William Watts Overseer of the Poor the sum of [fold] pound 11s in part of the money due me from Parish.

Elizabeth *(her mark)* W*[torn]* Teste: Richard Kesick

1800 – 1801 Entries

Elizabeth River Parish in account with John Holland Overseer of the Poor

1800	**DEBITS**	
20 Apr	Cash pd William Peaton for orphans	£1.10
24 May	Cash pd James Cooper for Dinah Cooper	£6
8 Jul	Cash pd Frances Millison for her children	£2
24 Jul	Cash pd Winifred Angel for her child	£2.2
26 Jul	Cash pd William Williams for Edward Dewier	£1.10
21 Aug	Cash pd James Cooper for Dinah Cooper	£6
26 Aug	Cash pd James Millison for burial of a man	£1.4
27 Aug	Cash pd James Peaton for orphan	£1.10
	Cash pd John Walker for Peggy Bental	£1.10
1 Sep	1 day attendance	6s
1 Oct	Cash pd Easther Cunningham	£2.2
6 Oct	Cash pd Fred Johnson for a coffin	18s
9 Oct	Cash pd Frances Millison	£1
14 Oct	Cash pd James Cooper for Dinah Cooper	£6
28 Oct	Cash pd James Peaton for orphan	£1.10
1801		
6 Jan	Cash pd William Thomas for Edward Dewier	£3
9 Jan	Cash pd Frances Millison for her child	£1.0.7
11 Jan	Hiring out the Parish Negroes	£1.4
14 Dec	Cash pd James Cooper for Dinah Cooper	£6
4 Mar	Cash pd Isaac Anderson for a coffin	7s 6p
	Cash pd William Ward for burying a man	£1.7.6
13 Mar	Cash pd John Walker for Peggy Bental	£2.5
13 Apr	Cash pd James Cooper for Dinah Cooper	£13.10
	Cash pd William Thomas for Edward Dewier	£2.5
	Cash pd Old Penelope for Grannying[17]	18s
	Cash pd for Stamp Paper	16s
	4 days hiring out the Parish Negroes	£1.4
	Cash pd Winifred Angel for her child	£4.10
	Cash pd Edward Valentine on account George Townsend	£6.15.6
	Cash pd the doctor for Parish Negroes	£3
	3 days attendance	18s

[17] The term most likely refers to Old Penelope serving as a midwife.

	Cash pd for coffin & burial Negro James	£1.4
	Commission on amount bonds and notes collection say £119.3.0 at 6%	£7.2.2¾
1799	**CREDITS**	
	Cash rec'd James Douglas for his note	£5
	Cash rec'd Mr. Campbell for his note	£3.3
	Cash rec'd Dr. O'Grady for his note	£4.10
	Cash rec'd John Dunn's bond	£22.5
	Cash rec'd James Douglas for his note	£10.10
	Cash rec'd J. Saunders for his note	£4.10
	Cash rec'd James Douglas for his note	£5
	Cash rec'd J. Saunders for his note	£4.10
	Cash rec'd Gilbert Robinson's bond	£12
	Cash rec'd John Dunn's bond	£11
	Cash rec'd Gilbert Robinson's bond	£12
	Cash rec'd Gilbert Robinson's bond	£6.15
	Cash rec'd John Dunn's bond	£15
	Cash rec'd James Douglas for his note	£3

Portsmouth Parish in account with Edward H. Watts Overseer of the Poor

1800	**DEBITS**	
10 Apr	Cash pd Mary Clemmonds	£6
	Balance due at settlement with the Court	£2.19.1
	3 days attendance at Court to settle (1799)	18s
26 Nov	Cash pd Ann Brown for board Stafford	£6.2.7½
11 Apr	Cash pd Charlotte Fiveash	£18.3.7
	Cash pd William Smith for waiting on Stafford	£4.10
	Cash pd Flauen for wrapping his leg	3s 6p
	Cash pd Tapley Webb for wine for him	13s 6p
12 Apr	Cash pd Mary McLenan	£9.12
14 Apr	Cash pd Zeby Kellum	£8.13.1½
	Cash pd Mary Combs	£15.15
	Cash pd Mary Blyth for Joseph Nunn	£7.8.6
	Cash pd Ann Eagles	12s
1 Aug	Cash pd Alexander Keeling for a coffin for Simmons	18s
4 Aug	Cash pd Elizabeth Wilkins for self and Thornton	£16.18.9
	Cash pd Ann Fitzgerald board Culpeper	£16.14.8
12 Sep	Cash pd Philpotts before his death	18s
	Cash pd James S. Mathews	£1.17
	Cash pd Nelly Berry	£9.9.3½
	Cash pd board & clothes Thomas Jones, orphan	£2.11.4½
16 Nov	Cash pd William Smith for digging John Culpeper's grave	4s 6p
	Cash pd Joseph Carter's wife	£14
	Cash pd James Duffee boarding & attending a distressed man	£1.8.6
	Cash pd for a quart wine for distressed man	3s

	Cash pd Mathew Howard	£22.10
	Cash pd Judith Rodman for Hannah Nunn	£9.7.7½
	Cash pd Elizabeth House	£10.10
	Cash pd Ann Wakefield for William Hare, orphan	17s 6p
	Cash pd Elizabeth Brown	£9.19.7
	Cash pd Elizabeth Kelly for Phillips	£1.16
	Cash pd Maurice Damron	£15.5
	Cash pd Letisha Rodman for Mathew Nunn	£5
	Cash pd Hopkins for making coffin for *[blank]*	10s
	Cash pd Caty Owens	£3.12
	Cash pd Elizabeth House	£1.10
	Cash pd Elizabeth Kelly for supporting Phillips	9s
2 Dec	Cash pd Mary Combs	£1.4
1801		
	Cash pd for a shroud for Alexander Phillips	12s
	Cash pd Mary Blyth for Joseph Nunn	£2.8.9
8 Jan	Cash pd Elizabeth Wilkins	£1.13.9
	Cash pd Elizabeth House	15s
31 Mar	Cash pd Mary Combs	£1.10
	Cash pd Mary Clemmonds	18s
	Cash pd Mary Carter	£1
4 Apr	Cash pd Maurice Damron	£1.4
10 Apr	Cash pd Lydia Collins	9s
	Cash pd Mathew Howard	£3
	Cash pd Elizabeth Wilkins Zibby Kellum	£1.16
	Cash pd Elizabeth House, Mary McLenan	£1.19
20 Apr	Cash pd Charlotte Fiveash	£6
1799	**CREDITS**	
	Cash rec'd Andrew Kidd, collector	£45
1800		
16 Dec	Cash rec'd Andrew Kidd, collector	£169.6
1801		
Mar	Cash rec'd Andrew Kidd, collector	£10.9.½
20 Apr	Cash rec'd Andrew Kidd, collector	£25.10

Norfolk County in account current with John Butt, Collector of the Poor Tax for St. Brides

1800	**DEBITS**	
	Cash pd Andrew Kidd per order	£60
	Cash pd William Bartee per order	£60.1
	Cash pd Jordan Marchant	£261
	Insolvents	£7.7
	My Commission at 10%	£43.3
1800	**CREDITS**	
	Collection of 1,644 tithables being the number taken this year	£431.11

Portsmouth Parish *[other half of page torn out]*

1799	**DEBITS**	
15 Apr	Cash pd Elizabeth Peak for '97 $4 for '98 2 per month	$22.00
	Cash pd 2 years rent	$10.00
	Cash pd Margaret Cason for 1797 & 1798 at 9/ per month to 26 Mar	$21.00
	Cash pd William Carter for 4½ months of Joseph Brown	$27.00
	Cash pd Mary Brown to 26 Mar for 1797 & 1798	$13.75
	Cash pd James Richardson 1 week Joseph Brown	$2.00
	Cash pd his funeral expenses	$5.80
	Cash pd Maurice Damron 1797 & 1798 to 26 Mar	$28.00
	Cash pd William Trigleth for Joshua Brown	$3.00
	Cash pd Theo Cherry for Argent Bennet and son 4 months	$24.00
	Cash pd Joseph Owens for keeping Peggy Richardson for '97	$24.00
4 Aug	Cash pd Margaret Richardson for Peggy Richardson 12 months	$70.50
	4 days attendance at meeting	$4.00
1 Sep	Cash pd William Plummer for 3½ months Peggy Richardson	$21.00
1800		
13 Apr	Cash pd Margaret Cason in full to this date 9 months	$18.00
8 May	Cash pd Stephen Anderson to 26 Mar 1800	$36.00
	Cash pd Maurice Damron 26 Aug 1799	$10.00
	Cash pd Jeremiah Cox for nursing & burying Joseph Carter	$13.13
	Cash pd William Wakefield for Margaret Cattenhead for 1798 & 1799 to 26 Mar 1800	$48.00
	Cash pd John Peed for nursing Elizabeth Peed 4 months	$20.00
	Cash pd for keeping 2 orphans of E. Peak	$66.67
	Cash pd clothes found Peggy Richardson 3 years	$13.33
	Cash due John Pollick for keeping Peggy Richardson 12 months	$50.00
1801		
	2 days attendance meeting of overseers in 1799	$2.00
26 Mar	Cash pd Stephen Anderson in full to this day	$48.00
	2 days attendance meeting of overseers in 1800	$2.00
22 Apr	1 day attendance meeting overseers in 1800	$1.00
	Cash pd Stephen Anderson for 1797 ($6 for 1798 - $3 omitted)	$42.00

1801 - 1802 Entries

Elizabeth River Parish in account with John Holland Overseer of the Poor

1801	*Debit side is blank except for amount brought forward.*	
1801	**CREDITS**	
	Cash rec'd John Robbins' bond	£12
	Cash rec'd Gilbert Robbins' bond	£6.15
	Cash rec'd James Douglas' bond	£3
	Cash rec'd Gilbert Robbins' notes	£13.10
	Cash rec'd John Robbins' notes	£15
	Cash rec'd James Douglas' notes	£6

23 Jun 1801 Capt. Nathaniel Butt
Mr. Charles Hodges has kept 2 of the poor children for 20s per month each from 9 Jan 1801 to this date which is 5 months and 14 days.
J. Marchant

The Overseers consider the demand of Mr. Hodges not legal. The within children having been commanded to be kept free from charge. It was therefore the province, we conceive, of Mr. Marchant to have seen them delivered and settled with Mr. Hodges for the time of his having kept them previous to the demand of Mr. John Prescott's wife.
[signed] The Overseers.

1802 - 1803 Entries

At a Court held for Norfolk County 17 Jan 1803
Nathaniel Butt one of the Overseers of the Poor of Saint Brides Parish returned the following list of poor orphans[18] to wit: Joshua Charles and Lovey Woodard, James Creekmur Ferebee, William Shadack, Tillit, whereupon it is ordered that the Overseers of the Poor of Saint Bride's Parish bind out the said orphans according to law.
A copy Reste: William Wilson, Jr. Clerk of Norfolk County Court

Portsmouth Parish in account with John Hardy, Overseer of the Poor

1803	**DEBITS**	
5 May	Order on Joseph Kinder, collector, in favor Ann Townsend for	£12.6
	Order on Joseph Kinder, collector, in favor Sally King	£7.16
10 May	Order on Joseph Kinder, collector, in favor Hilliary Etheridge	£7.10

[18] Apprenticeship bonds do not survive for 1803. All of them between Duncan in 1782 and Creekmur in 1818 are missing. Also did not find these children in the Minute Books or Order Books when searching in creating the book on Apprentice Records for Norfolk County. Therefore it is impossible to properly index these "orphans" – is there 8 orphans or 7 orphans as it is a combination or surnames and names which could be either surnames or given names.

4 Jun	Order on Joseph Kinder, collector, in favor William Thompson	£6.18
20 Jul	Order on Joseph Kinder, collector, in favor Joseph Thompson	£6
25 Jul	Order on Joseph Kinder, collector, in favor Anna Culpeper	£6
30 Jul	Order on Joseph Kinder, collector, in favor Richard Rose	£9
31 Jul	Order on Joseph Kinder, collector, in favor Ann Townsend	£12
5 Aug	Order on Joseph Kinder, collector, in favor William Yeates	£9
29 Aug	Order on Joseph Kinder, collector, in favor Mary Bowers	£18
	Cash pd Leisha Owens for Martha Powell	£9.1.6
	Cash pd Hannah Bruce for keeping Smith Stafford	£12
	Cash pd Elizabeth Wilson for keeping Jenny Elks	£9
5 Sep	5 days at meeting of the Overseers of Poor to this day	£1.10
1803	**CREDITS**	
	Cash rec'd of Alexander Grimes, collector of St. Brides	£30

At a meeting of the Overseers of the Poor for Norfolk County this account was examined and allowed by the Board and was ordered to be recorded. 5 Sep 1803
Teste: Andrew Kidd

1806 – 1807 Entries

Parish of Portsmouth in account with Andrew Kidd Overseer of the Poor

1806	**DEBITS**	
	Orders drawn on James Brown, collector:	
18 Oct	Mary McClenan	$8.00
15 Nov	Elizabeth Williams	$4.00
19 Nov	John Salisbury	$5.00
	Cash pd John Salisbury	$3.00
	Mary Brien	$2.00
10 Dec	Betty Brown	$2.00
15 Dec	Elizabeth Williams	$6.00
23 Dec	William Smith	$8.00
1807		
2 Jan	John Salisbury	$5.00
4 Jan	Mary Brien	$4.00
	Zibby Kellum	$3.00
15 Jan	Elizabeth Williams	$6.00
	Elizabeth Wilkins	$2.00
	Mary McClenan	$8.00
15 Feb	Elizabeth Williams	$6.00
18 Feb	William Smith	$4.00

19 Feb	Zibby Kellum	$1.00
23 Feb	John Salisbury	$5.00
24 Feb	Mary Brien	$2.00
15 Mar	Elizabeth Williams	$6.00
18 Mar	William Smith	$3.67
23 Mar	John Salisbury	$5.00
	Paid James Dawley's amount for William Johnson	$8.97
	Mary Brien	$2.00
2 Apr	Elizabeth Williams	$2.00
15 Apr	Elizabeth Williams	$6.00
	Zibby Kellum	$2.00
	William Smith	$3.67
18 Apr	Mary McClenan	$8.00
15 May	Elizabeth Williams	$6.00
	Paid James Johnson at different times	$2.50
	Orders drawn on John Pollock	
19 Jun	Mary Brown for keeping an orphan	$12.00
	Richard Kelsick for sundries furnished the poor	$31.06
	Pernel Pitt for sundries furnished the poor	$28.12
	Zibby Kellum	$6.00
	Sally Littleton for an orphan	$40.00
16 Jul	Tubman Laws for a coffin	$3.50

The Parish of Elizabeth River in account with James Dawley & Thomas Talbot

1806	**DEBITS**	
1 Nov	Benjamin Davis	2.00
4 Nov	John Grant's order to Thomas H. Parker	27.50
	Abigail Cooper for Peter Mason	10.00
12 Nov	Mr. T. Robbins in part for Peggy Hitchings	1.00
16 Nov	James Wakefield on account of Jane Richardson	16.25
17 Nov	Mary Davis in part of her claim	10.00
16 Nov	John Johnston's account against the poor house from 16 Aug to 16 Nov 1806	27.75
30 Oct	Richard Bailey for Judy Wright's coffin	3.00
	Digging her grave, paying John Grant, Sr.	2.50
19 Nov	Mrs. Williams for keeping Ellis' orphan	19.67
13 Dec	Mrs. Rockwell for Mr. Jackson	5.00
16 Dec	Benjamin Davis in part his claim	23.75
20 Dec	James Nimmo for 8 petitions & summons	10.00
	James Nimmo for 5% commissions on the above	2.10
	Paying Sergeant of Norfolk Borough for serving the processes	1.20
23 Dec	William Maye for keeping Peggy Hitchings a month	1.66
1807		
3 Jan	Thomas Robbins' account of keeping Peggy Hitchings	3.00
5 Jan	Mary Davis and paying blind Jack	4.33
27 Jan	Ann Cooper	14.14
29 Jan	Mrs. Rockwell for Mr. Fisher	5.00

30 Jan	John Guy for himself, paying Benjamin Davis	12.00
15 Feb	Benjamin Reynolds for clothing Negro Dinah	4.50
	Mrs. Paine and Thomas Robbins	16.50
	Benjamin Davis for Ben Reynolds and John Cooper	8.87
	Moses Langley for himself, paying Mrs. Rockwell	7.00
21 Feb	Mrs. Morse, paying Thomas Robbins	2.00
	William Langley, John Grant's order for keeping Edward Dwier	33.33
23 Feb	Abigail Cooper, Ann Cooper	7.67
28 Feb	Thomas Robbins for P. Hitchings, Mrs. Morse	9.00
	Joseph Hewett for keeping Hitchings' orphans	7.50
	James Wakefield for keeping Jane Richardson	8.75
7 May	William Fisher on account of Edward Dwier	3.00
8 Jun	Mary Davis, Abigail Cooper, Mrs. Morse	4.00
	Cash pd for Mrs. Paine & 2 children at poor house from the 4 Dec to 1 Mar 1808 including charges of sending her provision etc. and some articles furnished by James Dawley as account rendered	19.12
	Abigail Cooper for Peter Mason	2.00
1 Aug	Clerk's tickets to Samuel Moseley	12.39
	Clerk's tickets for serving process on Wilds & Blanchard 1805	.60
	Francis Petree for taking care of and burying James Lamb	5.00
3 Jul	John Ewell on account of Jane Richardson	20.00
	Joseph Hewett on account of Hitchings' orphan	6.25
5 Aug	David Fentress cash	15.00
	Andrew Kidd, Treasurer of Norfolk County, sum ordered by the Court to be paid to James Dawley for Mrs. Deal to be repaid by the said Dawley	24.00
	Mary Davis' claim for Hitchings' orphan	13.00
	Benjamin Davis order in favor of Mary Davis	4.12
	Dr. Balfour for finding clothes for Negro Betty	5.00
	Commission on $489.25 at 5% for hiring out the Parish Negroes, taking the bonds and collecting the money	24.37
1806	**CREDITS**	
	Frost's 3rd quarter for Negro	15.00
Nov	West for Billy Pugh $15, Leaton $17.50	32.50
	Collector Godfrey $10, West $6.25	16.25
	Martin $4.37, Ford $5.00	9.37
	Ford $5, Leaton $17.50	22.50

Dec	Leaton $17.50, collector Godfrey $10	27.50
	West	6.25
	James Nimmo for 2 judgement instruments & costs vs Bowdoin and Whitehead	35.34
	James Nimmo for judgement instrument & costs in a petition vs. John Wilds & Thomas Blanchard	21.30
1807		
	George Young $3.75, Frost $15	18.75
	Benjamin Reynolds 2 notes for Negro hire	14.75
	West for Billy Pugh	15.00
	First quarter of Dr. Taylor's note for Jasper	20.00
	West for Billy Pugh	15.00
	Collector William Godfrey's note paid William Langley	40.00
	Robbins first quarter for David	20.00
	William Maye for the parish land for 1806	10.00
	West's note for Billy Pugh	15.00
	Execution vs Wilds & Blanchard per Samuel Moseley	16.61
	$17.50 James Dawley charged himself with & is at loss how or whether he rec'd it	17.50
	Collector William Godfrey's note to J. Ewel	20.00
	West to Joseph Hewett	6.25
	Part of a judgement vs Wilds & Blanchard in 1805	5.00
	3rd quarter hire of Negro Jasper that will be due 1 Jan next	60.00
	Balance of Negro Betsy's hire from Dr. Balfour	5.00
	Amount of A. Martin's note paid by J. Johnston	4.37

At a Meeting of the Overseers of the Poor for Norfolk County 26 Mar 1808 Ordered that the Account of James Dawley balances be rec'd and filed the same having been examined by the board.

Teste: Andrew Kidd, Clerk

[torn] 1807 Parish of St. Brides

Thomas Tuley *[paper torn]*
Paid Jesse Hanbery for keeping of Nancy Brasey, one of the poor $10
Paid Charete Atkison for keeping of James & Lidey Sikes, a poor persons $30
Paid Thomas Taler for keeping of John Overton, a poor person $12
Paid Dine Stuard for keeping of Thomas Pollock, one of the poor $26
Paid Thomas Mannen for keeping Elizabeth Sikes, one of the poor $20
Paid Elizabeth Hanbery for keeping of 3 orphans, some of the poor $10
Paid Rubin Wood for keeping children, some of the poor $20
Paid Caleb Crickmon *[Creekmur]* for keeping of Aby Crickmor *[Creekmur]*, one of the poor $12
Paid Dr. Harding for dockerny *[doctoring]* of Nancy Brasey, one of the poor $41
Paid Dr. Harding for keeping for docktem *[doctoring]* of 2 poor persons John Oventin & Susanne Reede $11
Keeping of Nancy Timberly one of the poor *[smudged]*

[next page of same document]
At a meeting of the Overseers of the Poor for Norfolk County on the 1st Monday in September 1807
Ordered that the above account of Thomas Tooley, balanced, be certified to the Court the same having been examined by the board.
Teste: Andrew Kidd

1807 - 1808 Entries

The Parish of Portsmouth in account current with Andrew Kidd one of its Overseers

1807	**DEBITS**	
17 Jul	Paid William Smith	$4.00
17 Aug	Paid William Smith	$3.00
18 Aug	Mary Brown for keeping an orphan	$8.00
	John Salisbury	$5.00
31 Aug	Zibby Kellum	$2.00
	Paid Mary Bloxom (omitted)	$7.00
	William Johnson to aid him in getting to Tennessee, his residence	$30.00
	Caleb Hodges for noticing George Nicholson and his security	$2.00
	Maintaining Elizabeth Williams and 3 children 2 months, they being extremely sick	$20.00
	Ditto 3 children 1 month	$6.00
	Amount of tickets paid James Brown	$14.26
	Demsey Jones for a coffin	$3.00
	Samuel Hall for a coffin	$3.00
	Nicholas Wood for digging 3 graves	$3.00
	Paid for a pair of shoes for William Johnson	$1.50
7 Sep	Paid for sundries furnished James Duffee and wife (sick)	$.58
	Cash pd Elizabeth Williams (June)	$6.50
	Cash pd Old Phillis, a Black woman, 1 pound pork, 3 packs meal, and cash	$2.94
	Paid Nan Smith for Old Phillis	$.50
	Cash pd E. Williams for her supplies	$6.00
	Cash pd Mary Johnson per order	$5.00
	John Salisbury	$2.82
	My salary as clerk one year and finding stationary	$33.34
	5 days attendance	$5.00
1806	**CREDITS**	
	Orders drawn on James Brown, collector	$130.84
1807	Orders drawn on James Pollick, collector	$187.31
	Cash rec'd of George Nicholson, collector	$70.80

Parish of Portsmouth in account with Robert Tart, Overseer of the Poor

1806	**DEBITS**	
12 Sep	Paid John Pebworth an order on the collector for Samuel Brown	$40.00
15 Sep	Paid Elizabeth Creech for Jenny Elks	$30.00
11 Nov	Paid Hilliary Etheridge for Ann Isdel	$25.00
22 Nov	Paid Ann Townsend for William Townsend	$40.00
1807		
7 Jan	Paid William Yates for Lavinia Hogwood	$30.00
	Paid John Rose for Richard Rose	$40.00
27 Jan	Paid Elecia Owens for Martha Powell	$40.00
9 Mar	Paid James Dale for Cortney Culpepper and Elizabeth Culpeper	$75.00
14 Mar	Paid Mary Bowers for John Powell	$60.00
18 Mar	Paid Barnaby Carney for Sally Hilling's 2 children	$40.00
	Paid Joe Elmore and wife	$40.00
23 Mar	Paid James Spring for John Elks	$47.50
27 Mar	Paid Frances Dale for Smith Stafford	$30.00
	Paid to Sarah Warren for Nancy Browne	$12.00
	Paid to Elizabeth Ellis for Sabra Grifface	$45.00
	DEBITS	
	Orders drawn on James Browne and John Pollick, collectors	$594.50

The Commonwealth of Virginia to the Sheriff of Norfolk County Greetings You are Hereby commanded that 10 days previous to the next Court you inform John Cornwell, Maximillian Herbert and John Hodges, Sr. that they have been appointed Overseers of the Poor for the Parish of St. Brides in the said County of Norfolk and require them to appear at the Courthouse on the third Monday in next month and make oath that they will in truly and faithfully administer the said office. And this you shall no wise omit and have then those this writ witnesses William Wilson, Jr., Clerk of our said County Court the 28th day of May 1807 in the 31st year of the Commonwealth

William Wilson, Jr.

1810 - 1811 Entries

The Commonwealth of Virginia to the Sheriff of Norfolk County Greetings: We command you that you summon James Young, Barnaby Carney and Samuel Weston, Gentlemen, to appear before the Justices of our said County Court of Norfolk at the Court House of said County on the third Monday in this instant then and there to qualify as Overseers of the Poor for the Parish of Portsmouth. And this day they shall in no wise omit under the penalty of £100 and have them there this writ witnessed. William Wilson, Jr. Clerk of our said Court at the Court house aforesaid the 7th day of May 1810 in the 34th year of the Commonwealth

William Wilson, Jr.

At an election held at the Great Bridge on the 7th day of April the following persons were elected Overseers of the Poor for Norfolk County Saint Brides Parish: Maximillian Herbert, Caleb Wilson and Joseph Nimmo

The Commonwealth of Virginia to the Coroner of Norfolk County greetings: We command you that you summon Maximillian Herbert, Caleb Wilson and Joseph Nimmo, Gentlemen, to appear before the Justices of our said County Court of Norfolk at the Court house of the said County on the third Monday in this instant. Then and there to qualify as Overseers of the Poor for the Parish of Saint Brides. And this they shall in no wise omit under the penalty of £100 and have then there this writ witnessed. William Wilson, Jr. Clerk of our said Court at the Court house aforesaid the 7th day of May 1810 in the 34th year of the Commonwealth
William Wilson, Jr.

Norfolk County July Court 1810
Bassett Butt is by the Court appointed Overseer of the Poor for the Parish of Saint Brides in the room of Maximillian Herbert refusing to qualify and it is ordered that he appear at the next Court and qualify.
A copy teste: William Wilson, Jr.

1816 -1817 Entries

The Commonwealth of Virginia,
To the Sheriff of Norfolk County, greetings:

You are hereby commanded to summon Tatem Wilson to appear before the Justices of our County Court of Norfolk at the Courthouse of said County on the first day of the next term to qualify as Overseer of the Poor in Saint Brides Parish in the room of Willis Wilson who was excused by the Court.

And have then there this writ. Witness: William Wilson, Clerk of our said Court, at the Courthouse aforesaid the 27th day of May 1816 in the 40th year of the Commonwealth. By the Order of the Court. William Wilson

1817 - 1818 Entries

List of the Poor Norfolk County Annual Meeting 1817

Samuel Bartee's District	Per annum
Children of Prudence Nichols under 7 years of age, kept by her	$36.00
Rachel Reins, an afflicted woman, kept by Charles Cuffee	120.00
[blank] Nosay a child of *[blank]* years, kept by its mother	24.00
Nathaniel Butt a man blind and lame kept by William Nichols	120.00
Molly Butt, a poor woman, kept by Mrs. Holstead	36.00
A foundling (found in the road) kept by Mrs. Mansfield	48.00
John R. White's District	
Children of Zach Douge kept by him	72.00

John Johnston's District	
Hannah Millison, a poor woman	36.00
Molly Mead, a poor black woman	24.00
Gersham Nimmo's District	
Mary Tyler, a child of Sally 2 years of age, kept by her mother	36.00
Edward Cooper's District	
3 children of Bridget Twiford's under 9 years of age, kept by her	48.00
Andrew Kidd's District	
3 children of Mary Johnston: 1 lame, 2 very young	120.00
2 children of Mary Wood under 8 years of age	60.00
2 children of Mary Tumblin under 8 years	36.00
3 children Elizabeth Owens 2 of them twins	48.00
2 children of Sally Hogwood under 8 years of age	36.00
Sally Kay, a lame woman, and 1 young child	36.00
Mary McFall, 3 children under 13 years of age	72.00
Elizabeth Doran, a woman with palsy	72.00
Mary Wood an afflicted woman with a sore leg	24.00
2 children of Mary Williams under 8 years of age	48.00
4 children of Mary Hofler, one lame, 3 very small	96.00
Elizabeth Wilkins, a poor woman and aged	36.00

1819 – 1820 Entries

Edward D. Wilson, Esq

Please pay to Dr. Joseph Schoolfield (to whom the Overseer of the Poor are indebted) the sum of $200 which when paid shall be placed to your credit in the collection of 1819

M. Cooke, Agent Portsmouth 30 Nov 1820

1827 - 1828 Entries

At a meeting of the Overseers of the Poor for the County of Norfolk at the Parish House of said County on the first Monday in June 1828 being the 2nd day of the month

Present:
Dempsy Watts from Portsmouth Parish
William Cocke from Elizabeth River Parish
William Godfrey from Elizabeth River Parish
Israel Foreman from St. Brides Parish
James E. Wilson from St. Brides Parish

The board proceeded to the election of a President and the ballots resulted in the election of Dempsy Watts, Esquire who took his seat as such.

The board next proceeded to the election of a clerk when William P. Young was duly elected.

Augustine Blake, present keeper of the Poor House, was re-elected at a salary of $149 per annum.

Resolved that in future no allowance shall be made for the support of the poor persons out of the poor house, provided that aged and infirmed invalid, diseased persons requiring nurses and children under the age of 4 years may at the discretion of any Overseer of the Poor be provided for out of the poor house.

Latitia Grant is allowed $3 per month for the support (out of the house) of her child William Grant under 4 years of age and an orphan of George T. Grant.

Peggy Hanbury is allowed $5 per month for the support of her infant children William Thomas and Edy Smith Hanbury out of the poor house, which said children were twins and 2 years old in March 1828.

Elizabeth Bain is allowed $5 per month for the support of her children Rachel and Richard Bain orphans of William Bain, the former child 6 years old and the latter 4.

Keziah Williams is allowed for supporting and nursing Nancy Williams, infant orphan of Joshua Williams, from 1 Feb to 1 Jun 1828 the sum of $12 dollars.

Keziah Williams is allowed $3 per month for the support of Joshua Williams, infant orphan of Nancy Williams.

Elizabeth Mason is allowed $5 dollars per month for the support of her infant children, Elizabeth Susan, Caleb, and Mary Mason, orphans of Charles Mason, Elizabeth Susan aged 7 years, Caleb 5 and Mary 3 years old.

Arthur Harvey infant, who heretofore has been in the nurture and care of a black woman of Captain Henley's, is placed on the poor list to be provided for in the poor house, which said child is said to be the son of Benjamin Harvey.

Samuel Watts presented his account for beef amounting to $5.92 which was allowed.

Lovey Cofield, a poor woman, is allowed $3 per month for her support.

James T. Wilson presented an account for a coffin for Samuel Gray amounting to $4 was allowed.

David C. Williams' account for coffins for poor persons amounting to $11 was presented, examined and allowed.

William C. Beale account for coffin since the last annual meeting amounting to $17 was examined and allowed.

Dr. Joseph Schoolfield, physician to the poor house and Parish Negroes, is re-elected for the ensuing year at a salary of $175 per annum.

The Board then adjourned for want of the commissioner's books until the third Tuesday in the month, then to meet at William Portlock's in the Town of Portsmouth at 11 o'clock.

Signed

Dempsy Watts President
William Cocke
James E. Wilson
William Godfrey
Israel Foreman

Agreeable to adjournment the Overseers of the Poor for the County of Norfolk met at the house of William Portlock in the Town of Portsmouth on the 27th of June 1828

Present:

Dempsy Watts, President, from Portsmouth Parish
Richard Myers from the Portsmouth Parish
Israel Foreman from St. Brides Parish
James E. Wilson from St. Brides Parish
Talbot Guy from Elizabeth River Parish
William Cocke from Elizabeth River Parish
William Godfrey from Elizabeth River Parish

William Cocke presented his account for furnishing the parishioners at the Parish House with 100 cords of wood up to 17 Jun instant, for 300 pounds straw and for 15 days services as Overseer of the Poor in all amounting to $84 dollars which was allowed.

Sarah Myers is allowed $3 per month for keeping her daughter Susannah, which child is said to be a lunatic, the said allowance to commence on 1 Jul next.

Diky Bain is allowed $3 per month for keeping Margaret Ann Lane, an orphan child, supposed to be 5 years old.

Martha Wilkerson is allowed $2 per month for keeping her child, James, which child is 5 years old.

Courtney Turlington is allowed $4 dollars per month for keeping her 2 children, Margaret and Mary, the said allowance to commence this day.

Mary Ann Lowrey is allowed $2 per month for keeping her daughter, Mary Ann.

Frances Butt is allowed $2 dollars per month for keeping her child, Martha.

John H. Hodges of St. Brides Parish and Samuel Weston of Portsmouth Parish, Overseers, appeared and took their seats.

Ordered that the agent for the Overseers of the Poor advertise in one of the Norfolk papers to receive sealed proposals for rations to be furnished the parishioners in the parish house on or before the 27th of present month, each ration to consist of the following articles: ¼ pound of the middling of bacon, 3 half pints of meal, one ozen *[ounce?]* sugar, 1/3 ozen coffee and half a gill of molasses.

Ordered that William Cocke be authorized to furnish the parishioners at the Parish house with more for the ensuing 12 months the wood to be cut off of the parish land and to furnish the same at 67 cents per cord and that the superintendent of the parish house attend the measurement of the same.

William Cocke, Samuel Weston and James E. Wilson are appointed a committee to visit the Parish House once a month for the purpose of examining into the situation of the poor.

Ordered that the President of the Board of Overseers of the Poor be authorized to call a meeting of the Overseers whenever required by any one of the Overseers.

Adjourned to meet at this place on the 27th instant at 10 o'clock.

[Signed] Dempsy Watts, President
Richard Myers
Talbot Guy
Samuel Weston
William Godfrey
James E. Wilson
Israel Foreman
William Cocke
John H. Hodges

Agreeable to adjournment of the Overseers of the Poor for the County of Norfolk met at the House of William Portlock in the Town of Portsmouth on 27 Jun 1828

Present: Dempsy Watts, President, from Portsmouth Parish
Israel Foreman from St. Brides Parish
John H. Hodges from St. Brides Parish
Talbot Guy from Elizabeth River Parish
William Cocke from Elizabeth River Parish
William Godfrey from Elizabeth River Parish

Abraham Flannigan presented an account for maintaining Peter Waterfield, a poor man, and for furnishing a coffin for the same, which said account amounting to $10 was examined and allowed.

Richard Myers of Elizabeth River Parish and James E. Wilson of St. Brides Parish, Overseers, appeared and took their seats.

Amzy Hanbury presented an account amounting to $20 for keeping Thomas Griggs 8 months and for funeral expenses which said account was allowed.

John Collins presented two accounts, one for coffins and for burying poor persons amounting to $83 dollars, one other for conveying poor persons to the Parish House amounting to $8 dollars, both of which were allowed.

Mordecai Cooke, Sheriff returned a list of insolvents for the year 1827 comprising of 329 tythes at 5 cents per tithe amounting to $164.50 which is allowed.

Stephen Price presented an account amounting to $10 for keeping James Pullen, a poor man, and for funeral expenses for the same, is allowed.

William Dailey presented an account amounting to $7 for keeping Nancy Creekmur and for funeral expenses for the same, which said account is allowed.

Ordered that the agent for the Overseer of the Poor to pay to Peter, a slave, the sum of $2 for keeping Becky one of the Parish Negroes.

Augustine Blake, Keeper of the Parish House, presented an account amounting to $34.53 for making clothes, etc. for the parishioners in the Parish House which account is allowed.

It appearing to the board that Mary Ann Lowrey to who an allowance was made for keeping her child Mary Ann is not a residence of the County. It is ordered that allowance be discontinued.

Mordecai Cooke, agent, presented several accounts, one for cash paid away amounting to $1699.22, one for provisions, etc. amounting to $543.23 and one for account current, showing a balance in his hands up to this date including the collection of 1827 of $130.54 which several accounts being examined were allowed.

Mordecai Cooke settled his account as Sheriff and collector of the poor taxes for the year 1827 as follows:

Amount tithes for 1827, 4458 at 50 cents per tithe $2229.00
Insolvents in Portsmouth and Elizabeth River Parish $164.50
Insolvents in Portsmouth and Elizabeth River Parish $105.50
Commission on $1959 after deducting insolvents $195.90

List of outstanding balances

Hannah Gavitt, administrator	54.13
Frances Ann Stewart	41.03
E. Doran	3.25
Ann Roy	18.33
Susan Grant	3.00
Ann Hogwood	1.53
Mary Mills	1.67
C. Millar	44.00
Fanny Creekmur	28.08
E. Newman's estate	8.00
Mary Johnson	5.00
Catharine Birch	3.00
Nathaniel Butt by Nicholson	10.00
A. Hefferman	8.00
William Barnard	5.00
Isaac T. Ingram, late Overseer of the Poor	1.00
Samuel Hodges, late Overseer of the Poor	9.00
John Wilson, late Overseer of the Poor	11.00
Carey Weston, late Overseer of the Poor	6.00
Josiah McCoy, late Overseer of the Poor	9.00
Nathaniel Wilson, late Overseer of the Poor	5.00
William Ivy, late Overseer of the Poor	4.00
Solomon Charlton's estate	3.00
Messrs. Shield & Ashburn	1.00
Peggy Windham	12.00
John Collins	167.38
James T. Wilson	6.50
Sarah Myers	33.00
William P. Young	33.34
Josiah Taylor	1.00
Benjamin Nottingham	5.00
Latitia Grant	3.00
William Bruce	4.00
John Anderton	4.00
Tapley Webb	2.75

Annual Allowances	
Latitia Grant for the support of her child	36.00
Peggy Hanbury's children	60.00
Elizabeth Bain's children	60.00
Keziah Williams for Nancy Williams' orphan	12.00
Keziah Williams for Joshua Williams	36.00
Elizabeth Mason	72.00
Samuel Watts' account	5.92
James T. Wilson	4.00
David C. Wilson	11.00
William C. Beale	17.00
Dr. Schoolfield	175.00
William Cocke	84.00
Sarah Myers	36.00
Diky Bain for Lane	36.00
Martha Wilkerson's child	24.00
Courtney Turlington's children	48.00
Fanny Butt's child	24.00
Abraham Waterfield's account	10.00
Amzy Hanbury	20.00
John Collins	91.00
Stephen Price	10.00
William Dailey	7.00
Becky and children, Parish Negroes	24.00
Augustine Blake's account	34.53
Augustine Blake's allowance	149.00
Mordecai Cooke, agent, salary	200.00
William P. Young, clerk	33.33
Richard Carney, late Overseer of the Poor	10.00
John Collins, late Overseer of the Poor	17.00
David Routh	9.00
Tatem Wilson	8.00
Willoughby Foreman	2.00
Nathaniel Portlock	16.00
Elisha C. White	14.00
John Wilkins	9.00
Lovey Cofield	36.00
Probable amount for poor house, provisions, coffins, etc.	1,000.00
CREDITS	
Probable amount of Negro hire to receive	508.00
Probable amount to be levied for	2,357.23
Number of tythe for 1828	4,581
Probable amount of insolvents	451

The Board proceeded upon the above estimate to assess the poor rate for the year 1828 and accordingly assess the same at 62½ cents per tythe and that the Sheriff collect the said tax in service or Virginia money.

Ordered that the agent for the Overseers of the Poor etc. again endeavor to hire out to the best advantage the Negroes belonging to the Parish by giving notice in some public print of the day of hiring and by paying a constable to notify all said Negroes of the time and place of hiring and require their attendance. And if any of the said slaves do fail to attend on the day and at the place of hiring so advertised, the agent is hereby authorized to have them taken up and imprisoned and to inflict corporal punishment in his discretion or he may think the offence or offences deserve.

Proposals were received by the Overseers of the Poor from several persons for the supply of rations for the use of the poor in the Parish House but some of them not being advantageous and others requiring explanation, it is ordered that the President of the Board and the agent do make such contract for the object aforesaid as they may deem advantageous.

In all future requisitions made out for rations for the poor it shall be the duty of the Keeper to submit such requisitions to the inspection of one of the Overseers of the Poor to be by him approved and countersigned.

Ordered that the Clerk furnish the Court of the County with a copy of these proceedings within 30 days of this date.

Adjourned

(signed) Dempsy Watts, President
Israel Foreman
Talbot Guy
William Cocke
William Godfrey
James E. Wilson
John H. Hodges
Richard Myers

21 Jul 1828 The above is a true copy William P. Young, clerk

1828 - 1829 Entries

Annual Report of the Overseers of the Poor 17 Aug 1829

At an Annual meeting of the Overseers of the Poor for the County of Norfolk at the Poor House of said County on the first Monday in June 1829 being the first Monday of the month.

Present: Dempsy Watts, President Portsmouth Parish
Richard Myers Portsmouth Parish
Israel Foreman St. Brides Parish
Talbot Guy Elizabeth River Parish
William Godfrey Elizabeth River Parish

William P. Young, clerk, is continued as such and August Blake is also continued as Keeper of the Parish House at the compensation of the preceding year.

The following is a list of the number, name and situation of the poor in the Poorhouse to wit:

Ann Creekmur, old and infirm
Henry & William Creekmur children of Ann Creekmur, between the ages of 6 & 8 years.
Mary Harding, old and infirm

Susan Johnson, insane
Mary Mills, old and infirm
Elizabeth Stewart, old and infirm
Margaret Jordan, old and infirm
Sarah Tyler, old and infirm
Elizabeth Macklin, rheumatism
Lucinda Hoffler, decrepit
Polly Clark, decrepit
Cherry Price, decrepit
June Price, infant of Cherry Price age 7 months
Jane Fennel, insane
Jesse Fennel, aged 5 months
Daniel & Julia Cherry, between 5 & 7 years of age
Margaret Thomas & her son John and Arthur Harvey were discharged on 28 May

John H. Hodges of St. Brides and William Cocke of Elizabeth River Parish appeared took their seats.

The following allowances were made to the poor out of the Poor House.

Ann Freeman for her children, Miles & Thomas, $2 dollars per month each from 1 Jun 1828 to 20 Apr 1829

Jane Nichols for her children, Richard & William, $1.50 per month each from 1 Jun 1828 to 20 Apr 1829

Tempy Jordan $3 dollars for her present relief and $3 per month for the support of her 2 children from 1 Jun 1829 to 20 Apr 1830

Burwell Barbour $3 per month from 12 Aug 1828 to 20 Apr 1829 for the support of his brother, a blind man.

Margaret Britton $3 for her present relief and $3 per month from 1 Sep 1828 to 20 Apr 1829 for the support of her two children.

Martha Wilkerson $1 per month in addition to her present allowance from 1 Oct last.

Jane Barrington $2 for her present relief and $3 dollars per month from 14 Oct 1828 to 20 Apr 1829 for the support of her child, Sarah.

Mrs. Skully $2.50 for nursing and boarding George Higgins, a poor man, one week.

Jesse Ballentine $6 for supporting Jane Fanning, a poor woman.

Boush Nicholson $4 for nursing and boarding Owen, a sick man

Sarah Sneed $4 for her present relief in Jul 1829

James E. Wilson of St. Brides Parish appeared and took his seat.

Sarah Gibson is allowed $3 per month from this date for the support of her sister, a blind woman.

Latitia Grant $3 per month from this date for the support of her child, William, age 5 years.

Elizabeth Bain $3 per month from this date for the support of her child, Richard, age 5 years.

Elizabeth Mason $5 per month from this date for the support of her three children, Elizabeth, Caleb and Mary, between the ages of 4 & 8 years.

Martha Sikes $4 per month from this date for the support of her two children, Lucy Ann & William, between the ages of 2 & 5 years.

Hester Windham $5 per month from this date for the support of her daughter, Peggy, who is unable from disease to walk.

Dempsey Creekmur $3 per month from this date for keeping Courtney Etheredge, orphan of Simeon Etheredge, age 4 years.

Frances Butt $2 per month from this date for the support of her child, Martha, age 5 years.

Smith Gammon $5 per month from this date for keeping the orphan children of Peggy Hanbury, William Thomas & Edy Smith, twins, age 3 years.

Frederick White $3 per month for keeping Joshua, infant orphan of Nancy Williamson, age 1 year.

Frederick Creekmur $3 per month for keeping Mary Creekmur, orphan of Nancy Creekmur, age 9 months.

Ordered that Martha Green & Caleb Cain be received in the Parish House.

Ordered that $3 per month be allowed James E. Wilson for the support of Bridget, a black woman of 90 years of age, also $5 per month for the support of Fanny Cuffee, a woman of color.

Ordered that Ann *[fold]*man be allowed $4 per month from this date for the support of her two children Miles and Thomas who are between the age of 4 & 6 years old.

Tatem Wilson presented an account for making coffin for poor persons amounting to $20 which is allowed and ordered to be paid.

Proposals for attendance on and the supply of medicine to the poor in the Poor House and Parish Negroes were received this day under seal from the following individuals and approved by the board to wit:

Dr. William Collins	$125
Dr. Edward Balfour	$125
Dr. Robert Armistead	$160
Dr. Edmund Watts	$140
Dr. D.C. Barraud	$150
Dr. Joseph Schoolfield	$100

and it appearing from the above proposal that Dr. J. Schoolfield is the lowest bidder, is appointed to the situation of Physician to the Poor in the Parish House and to the Parish Negroes at the price of $100 per annum.

Proposals were also received for furnishing the poor at the Poor House with rations from the several individuals, to wit:

L. Sandford at 9½ cents per ration

William Ward at 7 cents per ration and it appearing that William Ward is the lowest bidder, he is appointed to furnish the rations as aforesaid.

Ordered that the agent furnish the Keeper of the Parish House with 4 water pails, 4 bread trays, 3 iron spiders with covers, 1 iron pot of 4 gallons, 1 club axe and one spade.

Sarah Sneed, a lame woman, is allowed $2 per month for her support from this date.

Sarah Myers is allowed $3 per month for keeping her daughter, an afflicted woman.

Ordered that the sum of $2 be allowed and paid to Martha Thoroughgood, midwife, for attending Cherry Price, a poor woman.

Col. William Cocke presented an account for furnishing some wood & straw at the Parish House to wit: 150 cords wood $100.50 and 100 lbs. oats straw $1.50 which is allowed and ordered to be paid.

Resolved that William Cocke furnish wood at the Parish House to be cut off the Parish land for the ensuing year.

Adjourned to meet at William Portlock's Tavern in the Town of Portsmouth on the 18th inst. at 10 o'clock A.M.

At an adjourned meeting of the Overseers of the Poor for the County of Norfolk at the house of William Portlock in the Town of Portsmouth on 18 Jun 1829:

Present:

Dempsy Watts, President
Samuel Weston
Richard Myers
Talbot Guy
Mathew Godfrey
William Cocke
John H. Hodges
Israel Foreman

Mary Arrington is allowed $5 per month for keeping her children, Milly & Elizabeth, between the age of 2 & 4 years.

Jane Nichols is allowed $3 per month for the support of her two children, William Jesse & Richard Henry, between the age of 3 & 5 years.

Ordered that the keeper receive Martha Wilkerson and her two children in the Parish House.

The following allowances were made to wit:

Jane Barrington $3 per month for the support of her daughter, Sarah

Diky Bain $3 per month for keeping Margaret Ann Lane, an orphan child.

Margaret Brittan $3 per month for the support of her child, William, age 3 years.

James E. Wilson of St. Brides Parish appeared and took his seat.

Ordered that Mary Johnson be allowed $10 for her present relief.

William C. Beale presented his account for coffins made for the poor who died at the Parish House amounting to $31, is allowed.

John Collins presented his account for coffins made for the poor who died out of the Parish House amounting to $39, is allowed.

Ordered that $2.62½ be paid to John H. Hodges for sending Caleb Cain and wife to the Parish House.

Ordered that David C. Wilson be allowed $3, David & Fanny Cuffee $1 each for burying Fanny Cuffee.

Ordered that $1.25 be paid Richard Myers for sending Molly Clark to the Parish House.

Augustine Blake presented an account for making cloth and for the poor in the Parish House amounting to $14.88, is allowed.

William Ward ration contractor presented his account showing a balance due him of $207.34, which balance is allowed.

Ordered that $5 be paid Talbot Guy for his services as Overseer of the Poor.

Ordered that $9.25 be paid Dempsy Watts for sending poor persons to the Parish House.

Adjourned to meet at this place on the 25th instant at 10 o'clock a.m.

At a meeting of the Overseer of the Poor of Norfolk County continued by adjournment and held at Portlock Tavern in the Town of Portsmouth on Thursday 25 Jun 1829

Present:

Dempsy Watts President
William Cocke
William Godfrey
Richard Myers
James E. Wilson
Israel Foreman
John H. Hodges

Mary Sikes is allowed $3 per month for the support of her youngest child, Edward Sikes, age 3 years.

William Fratis is allowed $2 per month for the support of Sarah Miller, the infant child of Barbary Miller.

Rebecca Haynes and John Henry Haynes, children of John L. Haynes, between the age of 3 & 6 years are to go to the Poor House.

Lucy Cofield, an idiot, daughter of William Cofield, allowed $3 per month.

Pursuant to an act of the last General Assembly of Virginia passed 20 Feb 1829 requiring the Clerk, Agents or President of the Overseers of the Poor in the respective counties of this Commonwealth to examine the records of their respective board and to report to the Auditor of Public Accounts in the form prescribed by the said Act all authentic information furnished thereby, respecting the number of the poor, the manner and annual expenses of their maintenance from 1 Jan 1800 to the date of said report. It is ordered that William P. Young, Clerk of the Overseers of Norfolk County be appointed to that duty and that he also make out and furnish to the auditor within the time required by law the report aforesaid.

List of outstanding balances due from the Overseers of the Poor to sundry person to wit:

Hannah Gavitt, Admin	$54.13
Frances Ann Stewart	$41.03
E. Doran	$3.25
Ann Ray	$18.33
Susan Grant	$3.00
Ann Hogwood	$1.53
Mary Mills	$1.67
C. Millar	$44.00
Fanny Creekmur	$28.08
E. Newman's estate	$8.00
Mary Johnson	$5.00
Catharine Birch	$3.00
Catherine Hefferman	$8.00
William Barnard	$5.00
Isaac T. Ingram, late Overseer of the Poor	$1.00
John Wilson	$11.00

Carey Weston	$6.00
Josiah McCoy	$9.00
Nathaniel Wilson	$5.00
William W. Ivy	$4.00
Solomon Charlton's estate[19]	$3.00
Shield & Ashburn	$2.00
Peggy Windham	$8.00
William P. Young, clerk (owed for 2 years)	$66.67
Josiah Taylor	$1.00
Benjamin Nottingham	$5.00
Latitia Grant	$3.00
William Bruce	$4.00
John Anderton	$4.00
Stephen Price	$10.00
William Dailey	$7.00
Smith Gammon for J. Hanbury's child	$5.00
Frances Butt's infant orphan	$2.00
Richard Carney, late Overseer of the Poor	$10.00
W. Foreman, late Overseer of the Poor	$2.00
Nathaniel Portlock	$16.00
Elisha C. White	$14.00
John Wilkinson	$9.00
Tatem Wilson's account	$20.00
William Cocke's account	$72.00
John Collins' account	$29.00
David C. Wilson's account	$3.00
David Cuffee	$1.00
Fanny Cuffee	$1.00
Augustine Blake	$14.88
D. Watts	$9.25
William Fratis for keeping Barbara Mills	$6.00
M. Cooke, bill of account to Jun 1829	$304.06
Overseer of Poor since Jun 1828 inclusive	$52.00
Annual Allowances	
Diky Bain	$36.00
Ann Foreman	$48.00
Jane Nichols	$36.00
Mary Britton	$36.00
Sarah Gibson	$36.00
Latitia Grant	$36.00
Elizabeth Bain	$36.00

[19] Solomon Charlton died before 19 Jul 1824 when Jordan Charlton was appointed his administrator. On 19 Feb 1827, John Wilkins was appointed the administrator for the estate unadministered by Jordan Charlton (Sharon Gable and Truitt Bonney, *Norfolk County Virginia (extant) Administrator Bonds 1711-1850* (Suffolk, Virginia: privately published, 2008), p 28.).

Elizabeth Mason	$60.00
Martha Sikes	$48.00
Peggy Windham	$60.00
Dempsey Creekmur	$36.00
Frances Butt	$24.00
Smith Gammon	$60.00
Frederick White	$36.00
Frederick Creekmur	$36.00
James C. Wilson	$36.00
James C. Wilson	$60.00
Sarah Sneed	$24.00
Sarah Myers	$36.00
Mary Arrington	$60.00
Levy Cofield	$36.00
William Frias	$24.00
Auge Blake, keeper	$149.00
Dr. Schoolfield, physician	$100.00
M. Cooke, agent	$200.00
William P. Young, clerk	$33.34
Rations, clothing, fuel, etc.	$1049.00
Mary Sikes' annual allowance to Jun 1830	$30.00
William Nicholson's allowance to Jun 1830	$84.00
CREDITS	
Probable amount of Negro hire	$600.00
Number tithes for 1829	$5689
Insolvents	-689
$5000 at 662½ - $3,125	$5000.00

The board proceeded upon the above estimate to assess the poor rate for the year 1829 and accordingly assess the same at 6½ cents per tythe and the sheriff is hereby appointed to collect the same.

Resolved that in future the keeper of the Poor House shall not be authorized to have cut or used in the said poorhouse or on the premises a greater quantity of fuel than 100 cords of wood unless he shall be authorized so to do by the written order of two Overseers of the Poor.

Ordered that the Clerk of this board furnish the Court of Norfolk County within 30 days with a copy of these proceedings.

Resolved that Richard Myers, William Godfrey and John H. Hodges be a committee to visit the Parish House once a month to examine into the situation of the poor.

Adjourned
William P. Young, clerk

1851 - 1852 Entries

Statement C
Returned with report of Overseers of the Poor of Norfolk County Apr 1852

NAME	FROM	TO	LOCATION	
Nancy Brown	Apr 1851	Mar 1852	at home	48.00
Mary Lake				36.00
Daniel Sparrow (colored)	Apr 1851			18.00
Nancy Cherry	Apr 1851			24.00
Elvy Ash (colored)	Apr 1851	Dec 1851		27.00
Ann Willoughby	Apr 1851	Mar 1852		48.00
Catherine Iverson	Apr 1851	Aug 1851		7.50
Nancy Curling	Apr 1851	Mar 1852		48.00
Anna Golden	Apr 1851			24.00
Amy Cooper	Apr 1851			48.00
Catharine Bright	Apr 1851			48.00
Martha Whitehurst				36.00
Penelope Heath				30.00
Jemima Jordan				30.00
Elizabeth Shelton				24.00
William Ward's 2 children			John Cotton's	48.00
Mrs. Sikes			W. Halstead	24.00
William Green			at home	56.00
Martha Smaw		Sep 1851		18.00
Sarah Stafford		Mar 1852		48.00
Melissa Sikes				60.00
Elizabeth Vickers				24.00
Annice Waller				24.00
Elizabeth Brumell				24.00
Lelia Layler				36.00
Lille Reynolds		Jun 1851		6.00
Nancy Waller		Mar 1852		36.00
Mary Lorey				36.00
Polly Grimes	Apr 1851	Mar 1852	at home	36.00
Anna Wright				36.00
Joe Lewelling (colored)				36.00
Thomas Wasp			Ralph Dixon	24.00
Susan Cherry			at home	58.00
Anna Curling				36.00
Nancy Garrett	May 1851	Mar 1852		22.00
Ann Myers	Dec 1851	Mar 1852		12.00
Henry Gammon	Dec 1851	Mar 1852		48.00
Elizabeth Cooper	Dec 1851	Mar 1852		24.00

Statement B returned Apr Court 1852
Tabular Statement Relating to Poor Persons received at Poorhouse

NAME	FROM	TO	EMPLOYED	REMARKS
Cherry Price	Feb 1833		knitting	
Sarah Tyler	Feb 1830		knitting	
Mary Barnum	Apr 1847		gardening	
Nancy Graham	unknown		nothing	partially blind
Paul Brown	Apr 1843		at school	
Sukey Harden	unknown		nothing	idiot
Zena Bailey	Oct 1850	Mar 1852		
Emma J. Barnum	born 12 Jan 1852			
Elizabeth Etheredge	Mar 1847	Mar 1852		
Betsey Macklin	1839			
Mary Onley	Jul 1847			partially blind
William Onley	Jul 1847	Apr 1851		
Jesse Bradshaw	Mar 1850	Aug 1851		
Hannah Etheredge	Mar 1847	Feb 1852		
Sarah Hall	Jul 1850		gardening	
Joshua Hall	Jul 1850			small boy
Mary Hall	born 21 Jul 1850			
John Scaff	Dec 1850		at school	
James Scaff	Dec 1850		at school	
Willoughby Bright	Jan 1851		paralyzed	
Francis Bright	Jan 1851		gardening	
David Bright	Jan 1851			small boy
Ann Ancel	Jan 1851		at school	
Lavinia Ancel	Jan 1851			small child
Huldy Ancel	Jan 1851			small child
Alice Ancel	Feb 1851	Mar 1852		small girl
Elizabeth Ancel	born 7 Feb 1851			
Lilly Reynolds	Jul 1851	died 13 Oct 1851		
Mary Gregory	Sep 1851	Jan 1852		
Joseph Manning	Sep 1851	Oct 1851		
John Pelt	Oct 51	died 12 Dec 1851		
Benjamin Borum	Dec 1851	Jan 1852		
William Robinson	Jan 1852	23 Feb 1852		
Lydia Ovelton	Jan 1852		knitting	
Catharine Ovelton	Jan 1852		knitting	
Sarah Saunders	Mar 1852		gardening	
Sarah Smith	Mar 1852			broken arm
Joseph Cooper	Mar 1852			small child

Latitia Scaff	Mar 1852		knitting	
Lucy Harris	Mar 1852		knitting	
John Forbes	Mar 1852			sick
Lewis Elliott (colored)	1838		sawing wood	

The Overseers of the Poor of the County of Norfolk in accordance with the provisions of Chapter 51, Sec 26, Code of Virginia make the following report:

During the year ending 31 Mar 1852 they have provided at the place of reception for the wants of 41 white and 1 colored in all 42 persons. They have assisted at other places than the place of reception 35 white and 3 colored in all 38 persons. The aggregate numbers having been 80 of whom 76 were white and 4 were colored. Their names with the other particulars required by the said Section will be found contained in the Tabular Statements Marked B & C returned here with as a part of this report.

The following is a statement of receipts and expenditures for the part year to wit:

RECEIPTS	
Work done at Parish House	2.73
Rent of farm	30.00
Interest on $3550 of 5 & 6% stock	216.36
Annual levy (not all received)	3,000.00
EXPENDITURES	
Sundries for support of the poor at Parish House	871.66
Clothing	168.66
Medicine and medical attendance	177.44
Keeper's salary	325.00
Servant hire	60.00
Incidental expenses	382.94

During the year the Overseers had to borrow $2,000 to meet demands on them for which they had to pay $42.72 discount at bank.

The amount required to meet the expenditures for the ensuing year for provisions, clothing, medicine and medical attendance, salary of keeper with the incidental expenses by levy will be about the same as last year which in round numbers we put down at $3,000

Thomas Webb
President

The Commonwealth of Virginia

To the Sheriff of Norfolk County

You are hereby commanded to notify John M. Foster, John W. West, Wesley B. Taylor, Alfred C. Wallace, William J. Denby, William Godfrey, George H. Dashiell, William W. Warden, and Iverson N. Hall that at an election held on 27 May 1852 they were duly elected Overseers of the Poor in and for Norfolk County.

Given under my hand at my office 9 Jun 1852

Arthur Emmerson, Clerk

At a meeting of the Overseers of the Poor of Norfolk County held on 20 Dec 1852, the following orders were made

Resolved that notice of the death of John M. Foster, Esq. one of the Overseers of the Poor be made to the Court of Norfolk County that action may be had to supply his place.

Ordered that the Court of Norfolk County be recommended to give to Samuel Fisk the keeping of the child for which he is now chargeable for the maintenance of, and that the President be authorized to inform the Court of this order.

True Copy: George M. Bain, Clerk

1852 - 1853 Entries

The Overseers of the Poor of Norfolk County in accordance with the provisions of Chap 51, Sec. 26 Code of Virginia make the following report.

During the year ending 31 Mar 1853, they have provided at the place of exception for the wants of 50 white and 6 colored in all 56 persons. They have assisted at other places than the place of reception 28 white and 2 colored in all 30 persons. The aggregate number having been 86, of whom 78 were white and 8 were colored. Their names with the other particulars required by said section will be found contained in the tabular statement (marked B & C) returned here with as a part of this report. The following is a statement of receipts and expenditures for the past year:

Receipts	
Balance in hand last report	$509.63
Work done at Parish House	$5.22
interest on $3550 of 6 & 5% stock	$216.36
Annual Levy none paid in	$3000.00
Expenditures	
Paid for sundries for & support of the Poor House	
For provisions	$911.36
For clothing	$176.30
For Medicine & Medical attendance	$253.83
Keeper's salary	$325.00
For cook	$60.00
For incidental expenses	$745.25
Paid for assistance to persons other than at Poor House - statement C	$958.45

The board have had to borrow money during the past year to meet expenses. Which will be paid out of receipt from Sheriff when in hand.

The amount required to meet the expenditures for the ensuring year for provisions, clothing, medicine and medical attendance, salary of keeper with the incidental expenses by levy will be about the same as the part year which is among numbers in part down at $3000.

G.H. Dashiell President

Report showing the number of inmates provided for in the Norfolk County Parish house during the year ending 31 Mar 1853. The date admitted and the date departed during the year and how they are employed.

Name	Admitted / Departed	Employed	Remarks
Cherry Price	Feb 1833	knitting	
Sarah Tyler	Feb 1830	nothing	old & infirm
Mary Barnum	17 Apr 1847	gardening, etc	
Nancy Graham	unknown	nothing	partially blind
Paul Brown	7 Apr 1843 – 11 Feb 1853	going to school	
Suky Harden	unknown	nothing	Idiot
Jane Barnum	born 12 Jan 1852 – died 12 Jun 1852		infant
Betsey Macklin	1839	nothing - will not do anything	
Mary Onley	26 Jul 1847 – died 21 Mar 1853		
Sarah Hall	30 Jul 1850 25 Oct 1852	gardening, etc	
Joshua Hall	30 Jul 1850 25 Oct 1852	nothing	small boy
Mary Hall	born 21 Jul 1850 - 19 Jul 1852	nothing	small girl
John Scaff	30 Dec 1850	going to school	
James Scaff	30 Dec 1850	going to school	
Willoughby Bright	4 Jan 1851	nothing - paralyzed	
Frances Bright	4 Jan 1851	attending to the helpless	
David Bright	4 Jan 1851	nothing – small boy	
Ann Ancel	10 Jan 1851	attending to the helpless	
Lavinia Ancel	10 Jan 1851	nothing – small girl	
Hulda Ancel	28 Jan 1851 – 29 Nov 1852	attending to children - small girl	
Lydia Ovelton[20]	16 Jan 1852	nothing	helpless
Catherine Ovelton	16 Jan 1852 26 Mar 1853	attending to the helpless	
Sarah Saunders	4 Mar 1852	nothing	
Sarah Smith	6 Mar 1852 – 21 Jun 1852	nothing	lame
Latitia Scaff	8 Mar 1852	attending to the helpless	
Joseph Cooper	9 Mar 1852	nothing	small boy
Lucy Harris	16 Mar 1852 20 Jul 1852	nothing	confined with a little one
John Forbes	29 Mar 1852 died 3 Apr 1852	nothing	
John Murphy	30 Apr 1852 died 6 May 1852	nothing	
Jesse Wallace	3 Jun 1852 23 Sep 1852	nothing	
Jane Rodman	10 Jun 1852 died 1 Aug 1852	nothing	
James Briggs	13 Jul 1852 – 8 Aug 1852	nothing	small boy
Andrew Briggs	13 Jul 1852 – 8 Aug 1852	nothing	small boy
Martha Garrington	22 Jul 1852 died 6 Feb 1853	nothing	sick all the time
Frances Garrington	22 Jul 1852 blank	nothing	infant
John Dobbs	24 Jul 1852 died 20 Aug 1852	nothing	sick
Louisa Perkins	11 Aug 1852 died 1 Jan 1853	nothing	confined with a little one
Elijah Etheridge	15 Sep 1825 31 Jan 1853	nothing	sick all the time
Copeland Pearce	16 Sep 1852 blank	nothing	bed ridden
Mary Lake	13 Oct 1852 30 Oct 1852	nothing	very old
Giles Nottingham	15 Oct 1852 blank	white washing the premises	
James Waller	26 Oct 1852 31 Jan 1853	nothing	sick
Zena Bailey	27 Oct 1852	knitting, etc	

[20] Most likely Overton as Ovelton is not a Norfolk County name, but it was definitely written as Ovelton.

Patrick Noles	3 Nov 1852	16 Nov 1852	attending to the sick	
James Sivels	7 Nov 1852	died 13 Nov 1852	nothing	sick all the time
John Caffry	21 Nov 1852		teaching & gardening	
Martha McCoy	7 Dec 1852		nothing	lame
Alice Ancel	born 7 Feb 1851			child
James Warrington	17 Feb 1853		gardening	
Robert Russell	18 Mar 1853 blank		nothing	lame

COLORED

Lewis Elliott	1838		nothing	very lame
William Warmey	23 Mar 1853		gardening, etc	
Mary Scott	16 Sep 1852	13 Dec 1852	nothing	lame
Rachel Foster	9 Oct 1852		nothing	very old
Lavinia Holladay	3 Nov 1852		nothing	partially blind
Wilson Hall	17 Nov 1852	6 Mar 1853	sawing wood, etc.	

31 Mar 1853
Nathaniel Manning, Keeper

Portsmouth VA 17 Oct 1853
The Court of Norfolk County Gentlemen
Here within I hand you a resolution paper by the board of Overseers of the Poor for this Court at their last meeting.
Respectfully George M. Bain Gentlemen O.P.

Meeting of the Overseers of the Poor of Norfolk County held 3 Oct 1853
Ordered that application be made by the Agent to the Court of Norfolk County for their consent to sell the present location of the Parish House for the purpose of buying more suitable place for the said House.
True copy George M. Bain Clerk

Tabular Statement C

Relating to Poor Persons assisted elsewhere, than at place of general reception
(format – name, two dates showing length of time assisted, where or with whom residing when assisted, amount contributed by the Overseers of the Poor)

Sarah Stafford	from Apr 1852 – Mar 1853	at home	$48
Ann Myers	from Apr 1852 – Mar 1853	at home	$36
Jeremina Jordan	from Apr 1852 – Mar 1853	at home	$24
Daniel Sparrow (col)	from Apr 1852 – Mar 1853	at home	$18
Joe Lewelling (col)	from Apr 1852 – Mar 1853	at home	$36
T. Wasp	from Apr 1852 – Mar 1853	at R. Dixon	$24
Amey Cowper	from Apr 1852 – Mar 1853	at home	$48
Cath Bright	from Apr 1852 – Mar 1853	at home	$48
Susan Cherry	from Apr 1852 – Mar 1853	at home	$84
Mariah Cherry	from Apr 1852 – Mar 1853	at home	$22.50
Nancy Brown	from Apr 1852 – Mar 1853	at home	$24
Mary Lake	from Apr 1852 – Sep 1852	at home	$18
Nancy Cherry	from Apr 1852 – Mar 1853	at home	$24
Ann Willoughby	from Apr 1852 – Mar 1853	at home	$36

Nancy Curling	from Apr 1852 – Mar 1853	at home	$48
Penelopy Heath	from Apr 1852 – Mar 1853	at home	$30
Nancy Garrett	from Apr 1852 – Mar 1853	at home	$24
Elizabeth Shelton	from Apr 1852 – Mar 1853	at home	$24
Calvissa Sikes	from Apr 1852 – Mar 1853	at home	$60
Virginia Revell	from Apr 1852 – Mar 1853	at home	$36
Nancy Waller	from Apr 1852 – Mar 1853	at home	$30
Mary Sorey	from Apr 1852 – Mar 1853	at home	$24
Margaret Snail	from Jul 1852 – Mar 1853	at home	$27
Mrs. Bonney	from Jul 1852 – Mar 1853	at home	$22.50
Mary Dews	from Jul 1852 – Mar 1853	at home	$27
Polly Grimes	from Apr 1852 – Mar 1853	at home	$36
John Whiting	from Dec 1852 – Mar 1853	at home	$24
John Ward's child	from Apr 1852 – Mar 1853	at J. Coltans	$36
Anna Golden	from Apr 1852 – Jun 1853	at home	$13
Allen Newton	from Apr 1852 – Jun 1852	at home	$6.45

1853 - 1854 Entries

The Overseers of the Poor of Norfolk County in accordance with the provisions of Chap: 51 Sec. 26 code of Virginia make the following report.

During the year ending 31 Mar 1854 they have provided at the place of reception for the wants of 51 whites and 5 colored in all 56 persons. They have assisted at the places than the place of reception 24 whites and 1 colored in all 25 persons the aggregate number having been 81 of whom 75 were white and 6 were colored. Their names with the other particular required by said section will be found contained in the tabular statements (marked B & C) returned herewith as a part of this report. The following is a statement of the receipts and expenditures for the year past.

1854	**Receipts**	
31 Mar	Received for levy of 1852 *	$3483.41
	Received for work done at Parish House	$6.71
	Received for interest on 5 & 6 % of stocks for 1853	$207.82
	Received for interest paid by Sheriff for delay of payments 1852	$58.84
	Expenditures	
	Paid for sundries for support of the poor at place of general reception viz:	
	For provisions	$988.52
	For clothing	$128.86
	For medicine & medical attendance	$283.25
	For Keepers salary	$325.00
	For cook	$60.00
	For incidental expenses	$1089.47
	Total at house of reception	$2875.10

	Paid for assistance to persons elsewhere than at house of reception as per statement C.	$431.11
	total expenditures	$3306.21
	Balance in hand +	$450.57
	*No parts of the levy received for the year of 1853	
	+ $1800 due to Portsmouth Savings Fund Society borrowed by order of Overseers of the Poor	

The amount required to meet the expenses for the ensuring year for provisions, clothing, medicines, medical attendance, salary of keeper with the incidental expense etc. by levy will be about the same as the past year i.e. $3000

Respectfully G.H. Dashiell Pres.

Report showing the number of inmates accommodated in the Norfolk County Parish house during the year ending 31 Mar 1854, the date of those admitted and departed during the year and how they are employed.

(Format: name, when admitted, when left, how employed)
Cherry Price Feb 1833 - blank knitting, etc.
Sarah Tyler 1830 - blank
Nancy Graham unknown - died 22 Jan 1854
Suky Harden unknown – blank nothing - Idiot
Betsey Macklin 1839 - blank nothing - will not do anything
John Scaff 30 Dec 1850 11 Jun 1853 going to school - small boy
James Scaff 30 Dec 1850 11 Jun 1853 going to school - small boy
Willoughby Bright 4 Jan 1851 9 May 1853 nothing - paralyzed
Frances Bright 4 Jan 1851 9 May 1853 attending to the helpless
David Bright 4 Jan 1851 9 May 1853 nothing – small boy
Ann Ancel 10 Jan 1851 blank attending to the helpless
Lavinia Ancel 10 Jan 1851 blank nothing – small girl
Alice Ancel born 7 Feb 51 blank nothing – small girl
Lydia Ovelton 16 Jan 1852 died 1 Sep 1853 nothing sick all the time
Sarah Saunders 4 Mar 1852 blank washing blank
Latitia Scaff 8 Mar 1852 blank attending to the helpless
Joseph Cooper 9 Mar 1852 2 Jun 1853 nothing small boy
Martha Garrington 22 Jul 1852 died 6 Feb 1853 nothing sick all the time
Frances Garrington 22 Jul 1852 blank nothing
Copeland Pearce 16 Sep 1852 blank nothing bed ridden
Giles Nottingham 15 Oct 1852 died 7 Jul 1853 nothing very lame
Zena Bailey 27 Oct 1852 29 Apr 1853 knitting, etc
John Caffry 21 Nov 1852 22 Oct 1853 gardening, etc sick all the time
James Warrington 17 Feb 1853 died 10 Sep 1853 nothing sick until he died
Robert Russell 18 Mar 1853 blank attending to cow
Christopher Columbus 2 Apr 1853 died 23 Jun 1853 infant picked up in Portsmouth
Elijah Etheredge 7 Apr 1853 28 Apr 1853 nothing lame
Elizabeth Trotter 8 Apr 1853 died 18 May 1853 nothing sick all the time
Thomas Trotter 8 Apr 1853 died 18 May 1853 nothing small boy
Joseph Manning 7 Jun 1853 blank nothing paralyzed

Mary Herd	11 Jul 1853	16 Jul 1853	nothing	very old
Lucy Harris	31 Aug 1853		attending to the helpless	
Georgeanne Harris	31 Aug 1853		nothing	has fits
James Liverman	10 Sep 1853		gardening, etc	
Cary Grimes	21 Sep 1853		gardening, etc	
Mary Stewart	14 Oct 1853	died 2 Nov 1853	nothing	sick all the time
Thomas Stewart	14 Oct 1853		nothing	small boy
James Waller	28 Oct 1853	6 Mar 1854	nothing	
			said he was not able to do anything	
Timothy Donovan	10 Nov 1853		nothing	a boy
John Donovan	10 Nov 1853		nothing	a boy
Ann Tomlinson	26 Nov 1853		nothing	says she is 86
Martha McCoy	5 Dec 1853	died 13 Dec 1853	nothing	sick all the time
Ann Miars	3 Jan 1854	died 27 Jan 1854	nothing	sick all the time
Mary Miars	3 Jan 1854	27 Jan 1854	nothing	small girl
Thomas Culpepper	4 Feb 1854	6 Mar 1854	nothing	lame all the time
Mallaby Butt	7 Feb 1854		nothing	sick up to this time
Colindra Murden	17 Feb 1854	22 Feb 1854	making her clothes	
Della Murden	17 Feb 1854	9 Mar 1854	nothing	too small to do much
Frances Murden	17 Feb 1854		nothing	small girl
Andrew Anderson	18 Mar 1854		nothing	lame
Edward Adolph	30 Mar 1854		nothing	sick & lame
COLORED				
Lewis Elliott	1838		nothing	very lame
Rachel Foster	9 Oct 1852		nothing	old & decrepit
Lavinia Holladay	3 Nov 1852		nothing	blind
William Warmey	23 Mar 1853		nothing	old & good for nothing
Peter Day	9 Aug 1853		nothing	old & helpless

"C" Tabular Statement

Relating to Poor Persons assisted elsewhere than at place of general reception[21]

Mrs. Harris	$5
Polly Grimes	$27
Catharine Bright	$30
R. Turner	$6
Mrs. Brown	$16
Amy Cooper	$32
Jo Lewelling, colored	$24
Mr. Sikes	$50
S. Cherry	$36
Mrs. Myers	$9
Mrs. Etheredge	$10
Ann Cherry	$28
Mrs. Jordan	$12

[21] The table is mainly blank. The items completed (names and amounts) are listed below along with 3 other fields... the first one Mrs. Harris is listed as being at home with the next two being ditto marks. The third one Catharine Bright, is listed as being Apr/53 and Apr/54 under the time assisted.

Mrs. Tonkin	$12
Mrs. Whiting	$24
Mr. Holland	$24
Anna Wright	$15
Mr. Walton	$4
Andrew Anderson	$8
Mrs. Patrick	$20
Mrs. Lock & Curling	$10.22
Marion Cherry	$5
Mrs. Ranhorn	$12
Mrs. Hall	$9
Martha Manning	$3

At a meeting of the Overseers of the Poor of Norfolk County held 4 Feb 1854

Resolved that the Court of Norfolk County be notified by the Clerk that Mr. Alford C. Wallace, one of the Overseers of the Poor, has moved out of his district and thereby vacated his office that his place may be supplied.

Copy teste
George M. Bain, Clerk

6 Feb 1854

I decree it due to the Court and Mr. Wallace to say that I have today learned that although Mr. Wallace's family reside near the head of the Western Branch yet at the same time he continues to do business at Deep Creek in the bounds of his district which the board were not aware of.

Respectfully, George M. Bain

1854-1855 Entries

The Overseers of the Poor of Norfolk County in accordance with the provisions of Chap: 51 Sec: 26 Code of Virginia make the following report.

During the year ending 31 Mar 1855 they have provided at the place of reception for the wants of 53 whites and 7 colored in all 60 persons.

They have assisted at the other places than the place of reception 21 white persons.

The aggregate number having been 81 whom 74 were white and 7 colored.

Their names with these particulars required by said section will be found contained in the tabular statement (marked B & C) returned herewith as a part of this report.

The following is a statement of the receipts and expenditures for the past year.

Receipts	
Balance in hand last report	$450.57
Levy of 1853*	$3526.87
Work done at Parish House	$10.69
Interest on 5 & 6% stocks 1854	$184.10
Rent of Parish Land	$60.00

William Brooks for support of servant Peter Day	$130.33
John G. Hatton one third of $3690 sale Poor House	$1230.00
Expenditures	
Paid for sundries for support of the poor at place of general reception viz:	
Provisions	$1024.69
Clothing	$112.16
Medicine & Medical attendance	$284.56
Salary of keeper	$325.00
Cook	$60.00
Incidental expenses	$1074.98
	$2881.39
Paid for assistance as per statement C	$409.00
Farm etc.	$2063.87
Balance in hand +	$238.30
*No parts of the levy received for the year of 1854 has been paid by sheriff	
+ $1800 due to Portsmouth Savings Fund Society borrowed by order of Overseers of the Poor	

The amount required to meet the expenses for the ensuing year for the support of the Poor of the County will be about the same as for the past year.
G.H. Dashiell President

Report showing the number of inmates accommodated in the Parish House during the year ending 31 Mar 1855: Admitted and departed during the year and how they are employed.

(Format: name, when admitted and when left, how employed, remarks)

Cherry Price Feb 1833 – 8 Feb 1855 knitting, sewing.
Sarah Tyler 1830 – 16 May 1854 unable to do anything
Suky Harden unknown – blank nothing Idiot
Elizabeth Macklin 1839 – died 29 Jun 1854 nothing very lame
Ann Ancel 10 Jan 1851 2 Jan 1855 waiting on the sick
Lavinia Ancel 10 Jan 1851 2 Jan 1855 going to school
Alice Ancel born 7 Feb 51 2 Jan 1855 nothing – small girl
Joseph Manning 7 Jun 1853 blank nothing paralyzed
Sarah Saunders 4 Mar 1852 blank attending to the helpless
Copeland Pearce 16 Sep 1852 blank nothing bed ridden
Robert Russell 18 Mar 1853 nothing confined to bed
Lucy Harris 31 Aug 1853 22 Jul 1854 attending to sick
Georgia Anna Harris 31 Aug 1853 died 13 Jul 1854 nothing small girl
James Liverman 10 Apr 1853 24 Apr 1854 gardening, etc
John Stewart 14 Oct 1853 7 Feb 1855 nothing small boy

Timothy Donovan	10 Nov 1853	3 Jul 1854	going to school	
John Donovan	10 Nov 1853	29 Nov 1854	going to school	
Ann Tomlinson	26 Nov 1853	died 5 Jan 1855	nothing	very old
Maloby Butt	7 Feb 1853	28 Feb 1855	gardening, etc	
Andrew Anderson	8 Mar 1854	5 May 1854	gardening, etc	
Edward Adolph	30 Mar 1854	25 Nov 1854	going to school	
Thomas Culpepper	12 Apr 1854	died 10 May 1854	nothing	sick
John Donald	18 May 1854	died 2 Aug 1854	nothing	sick
Frances Garrington	22 Jul 1852	29 May 1854	nothing	child
James Whitehurst	5 Jun 1854		nothing	sick
Deborah Darnel	10 Jun 1854	1 Jul 1854	attending to children	
Mary Darnel	10 Jun 1854	1 Jul 1854	nothing	small girl
Christianna Darnel	10 Jun 1854	1 Jul 1854	nothing	small girl
Martha Darnel	10 Jun 1854	1 Jul 1854	nothing	small girl
William Russell	22 Jul 1854	22 Aug 1854	nothing	lame
John Coleman	5 Sep 1854		nothing	small boy
Hiram Gleason	4 Oct 1854	28 Dec 1854	nothing	sick
William Trotter	10 Oct 1854		nothing	lame
Thomas Trotter	10 Oct 1854		nothing	small boy
Julia Cherry	30 Oct 1854	6 Feb 1855	knitting, etc	
John Cherry	born 24 Dec 1854	6 Feb 1855	nothing	infant
John Parker	8 Nov 1854	12 Dec 1854	nothing	sick
James Waller	22 Nov 1854	30 Jan 1855	gardening, etc	
Missouri Godfrey	29 Nov 1854	2 Dec 1854	nothing	small girl
John Cook	13 Dec 1854	died 10 Jan 1855	nothing	sick
Mary J. Stewart	13 Dec 1854		attending the helpless	
Robert Elderidge	13 Dec 1854	7 Jan 1855	nothing	idiot
Mary White	11 Jan 1855	14 Jan 1855	nothing	subject to fits
Jane Cox	18 Jan 1855		attending to helpless	
Wilson Cox	18 Jan 1855		nothing	small boy
Peter Cox	18 Jan 1855		nothing	small boy
John Ferebee	24 Jan 1855		nothing	lame
John Denson	30 Jan 1855	7 Feb 1855	nothing	dressmaker horrows *[?]*
Mary (unknown)	9 Sep 1854	died 11 Sep 1854	nothing	
Wilson Creekmur	7 Feb 1855	16 Feb 1855	nothing	lame
Mary Herd	6 Feb 1855		knitting, etc	
Charles Hargroves	12 Feb 1855	28 Feb 1855	nothing	lame
Nancy Garrett	5 Mar 1855		nothing	lame

COLORED

Lewis Elliott	1838	died 18 Oct 1854	nothing	very lame
Rachel Foster	9 Oct 1852		nothing	old & decrepit
William Warmey	23 Mar 1853	died 4 Aug 1854	gardening, etc.	
Peter Day	9 Aug 1853	died 9 Nov 1854	nothing	very old
Lavinia Holladay	3 Nov 1852		nothing	blind
Dorothy Sample	16 Aug 1854	17 Apr 1855	nothing	lame
Dempsey Ford	10 Oct 1854	died 27 Dec 1854	nothing	lame

Eber Shaw personally appeared before me, P.F. Outten a justice of the said County, and made oath that he would serve as Overseer of the Poor of the said County to the best of his skill and judgement.

Given under my hand this the 7th day of July 1855, P.F. Outten, J.P.

Statement relating to Poor Persons assisted elsewhere than at place of general reception

Note the "At Home" column is not repeated here. As with most of the forms, they filled in the first one, used ditto marks on the second and then nothing for the rest of the page, so they are all assumed to be "at home." Also omitted was the race column, these were all listed as white.

NAMES	FROM	TO	AMOUNT
Melissa Sikes	Apr 1	Mar 31	$48.00
Catharine Bright	Apr 1	Mar 31	$48.00
Anna Wright	Apr 1	Mar 31	$36.00
Mrs. Fowler	May 1	Jul 31	$9.00
Mrs. Tonkin	Apr 1	Mar 31	$36.00
Mrs. Patrick	Apr 1	Oct 31	$28.00
Mrs. Chitty	Jun 1	Sep 30	$12.00
Mrs. Newell	May 1	Mar 31	$22.00
Molly Etheridge	Jun 1	Jun 30	$5.00
Nancy Brown	Apr 1	Mar 31	$48.00
Miss Weston	Aug 1	Oct 31	$9.00
Polly Elliott	Sep 1	Mar 31	$21.00
Louisa Taylor	Sep 1	Sep 30	$5.00
Mrs. Williams	Nov 1	Dec 31	$10.00
Mr. Holland	Nov 1	Nov 30	$3.00
Virginia Rose	Oct 1	Dec 31	$6.00
Ann Ancel	Jan 1	Mar 31	$12.00
Mrs. Lake	Jan 1	Mar 31	$9.00
Mrs. Hoops	Jan 1	Mar 31	$12.00
Susan Cherry	Apr 1[22]	Mar 31	$25.00
Mrs. Burrus	Mar 1	Mar 31	$5.00

1856 - 1857 Entries

At a Meeting of the Overseers of the Poor held 19 May 1856

Ordered that George M. Bain, the agent of the board, be and is hereby instructed to apply to the Court of Norfolk County and ask that they make an order allowing the Overseers, their officers and the persons sent to and from the Poor house to pass the ferry free of charge.

Copy: George M. Bain, Clerk

[22] This appears to be a mistake as it should all be in one year and this is listing 13 months for $25.

To the Worshipful Court of Norfolk County

From the circumstances which surround Mary Elliott, from what I learned of her habits and character, I have no hesitancy in advising as Overseer of the Poor the bind out of her boys Arthur & Jack.[23] Arthur is supposed to be 12 years old and Jack 9.

10 Dec 1856 Josiah D. Miars, Overseer of the Poor

Filed with report of Overseers of the Poor
29 May 1856 Rec'd & Levy Made

Tabular Statement [C]
Relating to Poor Persons assisted elsewhere than at place of general reception
Norfolk County

Willis Wade	2 months	at home	6.27
Mrs. Williams	1 month	at home	3.00
Nancy Cox	2 months	at home	5.00
Harriet Woodward	2 months	at home	5.00
Mr. Williams & wife	2 months	at home	5.00
Polly Bonney	1 month	at home	4.00
Mrs. Ancel	5 months	at home	20.00
Mrs. Hoops	12 months	at home	41.00
Mrs. Sikes' child	12 months	Mr. Stewart	80.00
Anna Wright	12 months	at home	36.00
Dabra Darnel	12 months	at home	12.00
Catherine Bright	12 months	at home	48.00
Mrs. Bowers	12 months	at home	40.00
Mrs. Lake	3 months	at home	9.00
Mrs. Chitty	7 months	at home	21.00
Polly Elliott	9 months	at home	27.00
Mrs. Turney	12 months	at home	36.00
Mrs. Long	2 months	at home	6.00
Mrs. Cherry	5 months	at home	15.00
Mrs. Fry	5 months	at home	15.00
Mrs. Burney	5 months	at home	15.00
Mrs. Powers	4 months	at home	12.00
Mrs. Rose	4 months	at home	12.00
Mrs. Tonkin	4 months	at home	12.00
Mrs. Hayden	4 months	at home	12.00
Mrs. Stewart	3 months	at home	9.00
Mrs. Brittingham	5 months	at home	15.00
Mrs. Brown	4 months	at home	12.00
Mrs. Stublin	3 months	at home	9.00

[23] Jack was bound out to Thomas Grimes by the court on 29 Dec based on an order dated 15 Dec 1856. Jack is listed as a free person of color and the master who accepted him to learn the trade of a farmer was to pay $50 per annum after Jack arrived at age 10 with 25% of that money going to the mother if she was still alive. This order (to bind him out) was rescinded and annulled on 25 Jun 1857 (source original bonds at State Archives in Richmond).

Mrs. Jordan	2 months	at home	6.00
Mrs. Green	1 months	at home	2.00
Miss King	1 months	at home	2.00
Mrs. Herd	2 months	at home	8.00
Mr. Roach	2 months	at home	4.00
Daniel Sparrow	12 months	colored	62.00

1857 - 1858 Entries

The Overseers of the Poor of Norfolk County in accordance with the provision of Chapter 51 Section 2B Code of Virginia make the following report:

During the year ending 31st of March 1858 they have provided at the place of reception for the wants of 42 whites and 2 colored in all 44 persons. They have assisted at other places than the place of reception of 34 whites and 1 colored in all 35 persons. The aggregate number having been 79 of whom 76 were white and 3 were colored. Their names with other particulars required by said section will be found contained in the tabular statement (marked B & C) returned herewith as part of their report.

The following is a statement of the receipts and expenditures for the year past.

RECEIPTS	
Balance last report	$238.30
In part for levy of 1854	$3849.16
Vegetables etc sold from Poor House	$41.45
Interest on 5 & 6% stocks	$237.04
Rent of Parish land	$25.00
Balance sale of Poor House to J.G. Hatton 2/3 of $3690	$2460.00
Interest same	$53.71
EXPENDITURES	
Paid for sundries for support of Poor at place of general reception Viz.	
For provisions	$822.94
For clothes	$35.20
For medicine & medical attendance	$83.29
For Keepers salary	$243.75
For servants hire	$50.00
Incidental expenditures	599.95
Paid for assistance to persons elsewhere than at house of reception as per statement C.	$606.27
For building Poor House & farming implements	$3,513.49

*42.86 due for 1854 and all the levy of 1855.

+ Bill due and unpaid not rendered sufficient to consume the balance in hand

There is due the Portsmouth Savings Fund Society $1800 and to W.G. Britton $1566.67 balance for building the poor house which two sums will about consume the levy of 1855 when paid in.

The amount required to meet the expenditures for the ensuing year will be about $2500 or two thirds of what the levy for the past year was.

Respectfully,
G.H. Dashiell, President

The Overseers of the Poor of Norfolk County in accordance with the provisions of Chapter 51 Section 26 code of Virginia make the following report.

During the year ending 31 Mar 1857 they have provided at the place of reception for the wants of 28 white and 4 colored in all 32 persons. They have assisted at the other places than the place of reception 118 white and 1 colored in all 119 persons. The aggregate number having 151 of whom 146 were white and 5 were colored. Their names with other particulars required by said section will be found containing in the tabular statement (marked B & C) returned here with as part of this report.

The following is a statement of the receipts and expenditures for the year past.

Receipts	
Balance in hand last year	$749.77
From Arthur Emmerson being the amount deposit in Court in his hand by the Albemarle & Chesapeake Canal Company to be paid the Overseers of the Poor for damages to their land condemned for said Canal Co.	$170.00
Interest on 5 & 6% of stocks	$262.65
Balance levy of 1854	$42.86
Levy of 1855	$3339.49
Borrowed from Bank of VA	$1566.66
Borrowed from Portsmouth Savings Fund Society	$1500.00
Part of levy of 1856	$800.00
Sales of pork, etc. from farm	$51.81
Expended	
Paid for sundries for support of the Poor at place of general reception	
Provisions	$709.30
Clothing	$99.86
Coffins	$215.00
Keeper of Poor House	$376.91
Incidental expenses	687.03
Total at house of reception	$2088.10
Servant hire	$50.00
Medicine & medical attention	$158.91
Other than at place of general reception	$2445.50
For improvement on farm & balance for building	$1805.15
Debt in Bank of Virginia	$1566.66

The amount required for the ensuing year to pay off the debt due the Portsmouth Savings Fund Society of $3300 and outstanding bills due and unpaid of about $800 together with the amount necessary for the support of the poor in and out of the place of general reception is in round numbers about $6500 equal to a levy of $1.50 per tithe which the board of Overseers of the Poor respectfully recommend the Court to make the levy.

At a meeting of the Overseers of the Poor of Norfolk County held 11 Apr 1857
Resolved that the President of the board on making his report to the Court of Norfolk County for the year, ask that the court pass an order requiring the sheriff to settle his account for the collection of poor rates or County levy on or before the first of January of every year; as under the present arrangement the Overseers are put to considerable inconvenience by the delay of payments. See code of Virginia, page 280, Chapter 53, Section 16.
Respectfully W. Watts, President

Statement C
Tabular Statement relating to Poor Persons assisted elsewhere than at the place of general reception

(The race column was omitted as all of the people on this list were white. Also if the length is not noted, it because it was it was blank on the form)

NAMES	LENGTH	WHERE	AMOUNT
Nancy Cherry	2 months	at home	$5.00
Nash Cotton	ditto	ditto	$5.00
Mrs. Williams			$5.00
Poor man name unknown		Mr. Hyslip's	$9.00
Mrs. Stoakes		at home	$5.00
Polly Bonney	12 months		$36.00
Catherine Bright			$48.00
Joseph Roach			$33.00
J.M. Sikes			$60.00
Benedie Knott	1 month		$4.00
Mrs. Tinney	2 months		$20.00
Mrs. Hoops	12 months		$36.00
Mrs. Stublin	11 months		$33.00
Mary Herd	1 month		$4.00
Josephine Chitts	12 months		$36.00
Mrs. Powers	9 months		$45.00
Mary Barron	9 months		$54.00
Nancy Cox	12 months		$30.50
Mrs. Tonkin			$36.00
Mrs. Brittingham			$55.00
Mrs. Cherry			$54.00
Mrs. Hayden			$52.00
Mrs. Fry			$45.00
Anna Wright			$33.00
Mary Holden			$33.00
Mrs. Jordan			$54.00

Mrs. Bowers	4 months		$12.00
J. Nelson	2 months		$8.00
Mary Hickerson	12 months		$37.00
H. Powers	4 months		$12.00
Mrs. King	12 months		$27.00
Rosa McManis	9 months		$27.00
Mrs. West			$27.00
Mrs. Tremor			$30.00
Mrs. Broughton			$24.00
Mrs. Scaff			$24.00
Mrs. Tinney	12 months		$36.00
Mrs. Bowers			$36.00
Mary Hughes	9 months		$27.00
Mary O'Rooke			$45.00
Wabley Walsh			$15.00
M. Sullivan			$27.00
C. Sullivan			$27.00
M. Corne			$27.00
B. Naughton			$45.00
M. Currin			$27.00
Mrs. Keady			$27.00
Ann Dunkin			$24.00
Virginia Rose			$27.00
M.B. Perkins			$45.00
Lydia Pebworth			$45.00
M. McDorland			$36.00
M. Weston			$27.00
M. Godfrey			$27.00
R. Godfrey			$24.00
Ann McBride			$24.00
Mary Miskel			$27.00
Miss White	1 month		$3.00
Sarah Graham	8 months		$24.00
M. Barber			$24.00
Elizabeth Marshall			$24.00
Sarah Cocke			$24.00
N. Cole	8 months	at home	$24.00
Frances Newton	7 months		$21.00
Mary Stoakes			$21.00
Cath Herd			$21.00
Pamelia Miars	6 months		$18.00
Drucilla Willey	4 months		$12.00
Sarah O. Donald	6 months		$18.00
B. Kelly			$18.00
Eliz Brown			$18.00
S. Turner			$18.00
E. Ponneter			$18.00
C. Manning			$18.00

E. Williams			$10.00
R. Grimes	5 months		$15.00
Mrs. Richardson			$15.00
Mary Ann White			$15.00
Mrs. Garrison			$15.00
Mary King			$10.00
Mrs. Hunley	1 month		$5.00
Mary Herd	5 months		$15.00
Mrs. Knight			$15.00
Eliza Anderton			$12.50
Julia Thomas			$12.50
Mary Whiting	4 months		$12.00
Mrs. Shannon	2 months		$8.00
M.E. Louis	4 months		$12.00
Eliza Etheridge			$12.00
Mary Barsoline			$12.00
Lucy Godwin			$12.00
Mary Elliott	5 months		$15.00
Mrs. Manning	1 month		$5.00
Mrs. O'Neill	5 months		$15.00
Mrs. Hunter	2 months		$6.00
Sarah Martin	1 month		$3.00
Mary Brown	3 months		$9.00
Mrs. Harrison	5 months		$15.00
E.R. King	2 months		$6.00
Patsey Nelms	2 months		$6.00
Mr. Stafina	1 month		$2.00
Sarah Malcome	3 months		$9.00
Mrs. Bain	2 months		$6.00
Mrs. Etheridge			$6.00
Sarah Yates			$6.00
Mrs. Manning	1 month		$3.00
Sarah Payne	2 months		$6.00
Martha Davis	1 month		$3.00
Mrs. Hines			$3.00
Eliza Sikes			$3.00
Mary Bullock			$3.00
Mrs. Barber			$3.00
Nancy Brooks			$3.00
Ann Smith			$3.00
Nancy Garnett			$2.00
Daniel Sparrow (colored)	12 months		$69.00

Report of Overseers of the Poor to the Court Statement C.
18 May 1857 returned and filed with report.

Report showing the number of inmates accommodated in the Norfolk County Parish House ending 31 Mar 1857, the date of those admitted & departed the year and how they were employed and deaths.

William Jones	blank - 24 Jun 1856	gardening	
Nancy Garrett	blank - 31 Jun 1856	sewing	
Alice Morrisfield	blank - died 4 Mar 1857	knitting	
Lucy Harris	blank - 30 Jun 1856	knitting	
Polly Herd	blank - 15 Nov 1856	knitting	
Jane Hines	blank - 28 Nov 1856	knitting	
Adam Buschel			idiot
Sarah Saunders	blank -	washing	idiot
Thomas Trotter	blank - 11 Jan 1857	going to school	small boy
Frances Hines	blank - 15 Nov 1856	going to school	small girl
Emmy Hines	blank - 15 Nov 1856	going to school	small girl
William Tally	8 Jul 1856 – 6 Aug 1856	doing nothing	
Ann Tally	8 Jul 1856 -		
John Parker	25 Jul 1856 – 27 Jan 1857		
Joseph Ashton	26 Jul 1856 – 4 Aug 1856		idiot
John Collehon	30 Jul 1856 – died 5 Aug 1856		
Laurence Sutton	31 Jul 1856 – 2 Aug 1856	doing nothing	
John Glenard	7 Aug 1856 – died 10 Aug 1856		
Harriet Woodard	2 Sep 1856 -	sewing	
Robert Day	5 Sep 1856 – 7 Sep 1856		boy
John Welsh	2 Dec 1856 – 19 Feb 1857	doing nothing	
Thomas Brown	2 Jan 1857 –	doing nothing	
James Peed	5 Jan 1857 –	doing nothing	
Mary Barnum	7 Jan 1857 -	assisting the cook	
Joshua Hodges	6 Feb 1857 –	doing nothing	
Ann Dunkin	7 Feb 1857 –		
John Dunkin	7 Feb 1857 –	going to school	small boy
John Flynn	20 Feb 1857 –	doing nothing	
Emma Robinson, colored –18 Mar 1857 -		doing nothing	
Elizabeth Robinson, colored – 18 Mar 1857		doing nothing	small girl
Daniel Sparrow, colored – 30 Mar 1857		doing nothing	
Dorita Sparrow, colored – 30 Mar 1857		doing nothing	

Respectfully, David Lynch, keeper

At a meeting of the Overseers of the Poor of Norfolk County held 11 Apr 1857 Resolved that the President of the board on making his report to the Court of Norfolk County for the year. Ask that the Court pass an order requiring the Sheriff to settle his account for the collection of Poor rates in county levy on or before the 1st day of January of every year as under the present management the Overseers are put to considerable inconvenience by the delay in payments.
See Code of Virginia Page 280 Chapter 53 Section 16
W. Watts Overseer

Norfolk County 5 Dec 1857
Extract from the Journal of the Overseers of the Poor of Norfolk County at a meeting held 5 Dec 1857
Ordered that the Agent inform the Court of Norfolk County of the death of Winchester Watts, Esquire one of the Overseers of the Poor and ask that they order an election to supply his place. And remind the Court that the vacancy occasioned by the removal of B.H. Williams from his District has not yet been filled. Notification of which was furnished the Court at its April term 1857

George M. Bain Clerk and Agent

Personally appeared before me, Robert Dickson a Justice of the Peace in and for the County of Norfolk, William White who has been duly elected an Overseer of the Poor for the County of Norfolk in the fourth District in place of Blackston K. Williams who removed from his district at an election held on 9 Jan 1858 pursuant to an order of the Norfolk County Court who took the oath of fidelity to the Commonwealth, the oath to support the Constitution of the United States, the oath against dueling and the oath of office.

Given under my hand and seal this 16 Jan 1858
Robert Dickson, J.P.

[C] Tabular Statement

Relating to Poor Persons assisted elsewhere than at the place of general reception.
(all were provided for at home unless otherwise noted)

Polly Bonney	10 months		$40.00
Joseph Roach	12 months	R.H. Roach	$50.25
W.W. Carney	1 month		$5.00
Henry Thompson	8 months		$31.00
Nancy Cox	12 months		$24.00
J.M. Sikes	9 months	Mr. Sikes	$45.00
Catherine Bright	4 months	Mrs. Bright	$16.00
Mrs. Stafford	1 month		$4.00
Mrs. C. Harris	3 months		$9.00
Mrs. M. Conner	5 months		$15.00
Mrs. F. Brown	5 months		$15.00
Mrs. T. Chitty	5 months		$25.00
Mrs. D. Curling	3 months		$6.00
Mrs. M. Money	5 months		$19.00
Mrs. W.H. Stoakes	3 months		$9.00
Mrs. S. Paine	4 months		$12.00
Mrs. C. Manning	5 months		$17.00
Mrs. S. Yates	5 months		$19.00
Mrs. C. Herd	5 months		$15.00
Mrs. M. King	5 months		$15.00
Mrs. M.E. Long	5 months		$19.00
Mrs. M. Depety	1 month		$3.00
Mrs. S. Bain	3 months		$9.00

Mrs. Anna Wright	5 months		$17.00
Mrs. R. Godfrey	5 months		$19.00
Mrs. E. Sikes	3 months		$9.00
Mrs. Pebworth	3 months		$15.00
Mrs. M. Barber	5 months		$15.00
Mrs. E. Martial	5 months		$15.00
Mrs. Hoops	5 months		$17.00
Mrs. N. Brooks	5 months		$15.00
Mrs. B. Kelly	3 months		$9.00
Mrs. E. Powers	5 months		$15.00
Mrs. W. Brittingham	5 months		$25.00
Mrs. Rosa McManis	5 months		$19.00
Mrs. Richardson	3 months		$9.00
Mrs. Stublin	5 months		$17.00
Mrs. M. Hughes	5 months		$15.00
Mrs. O'Neill	5 months		$25.00
Mrs. M. Miskel's child	5 months		$15.00
Mrs. Brown & child	5 months		$25.00
Mrs. Frey	5 months		$15.00
Mrs. E. Etheredge	5 months		$15.00
Mrs. F. Newton	5 months		$17.00
Mrs. G. Rose	5 months		$17.00
Mrs. L. Gregory	5 months		$17.00
Mrs. M. Davis	3 months		$9.00
Mrs. Ann Willoughby	2 months		$10.00
Mrs. R. Grimes	3 months		$9.00
Mrs. M.A. White	5 months		$17.00
Mrs. E. Balance	3 months		$15.00
Mrs. M. Heyden	5 months		$25.00
Mrs. E. Deal	5 months		$17.00
Mrs. J.A. Broughton	3 months		$9.00
Mrs. E. King	3 months		$6.00
Mrs. P. Nelson	3 months		$6.00
Mrs. M. West	5 months		$15.00
Mrs. Thompkins	5 months		$15.00
Mrs. Price	1 month		$2.00
Mrs. L. Bowers	5 months		$20.00
Mrs. M.A. Whitting	3 months		$9.00
Mrs. M. O'Roke	5 months		$19.00
Mrs. E. Etheredge	3 months		$9.00
Mrs. G. Chally etc.	3 months		$9.00
Mrs. S. Cocke	3 months		$9.00
Mrs. M. Kady	5 months		$15.00
Mrs. M. Currin	5 months		$15.00
Mrs. M. Fulleran	5 months		$17.00
Mrs. Toole	5 months		$25.00
Mrs. Ann Gallilee	5 months		$15.00
Mrs. A. Sullivan	5 months		$15.00

Mrs. Ann Smith	5 months		$9.00
Mrs. N. Linscott	5 months		$14.00
Mrs. J. Thomas	3 months		$7.50
Mrs. M. Anderton	3 months		$7.50
Mrs. Perkins	5 months		$25.00
Mrs. M. McDonaugh	5 months		$25.00
Mrs. M. Weston	3 months		$9.00
Mrs. Gregory	5 months		$15.00
Mrs. M. Hickerson	5 months		$25.00
Mrs. B. McNelly	3 months		$15.00
Mrs. M. Holden	5 months		$17.00
Mrs. M. Wels	7 months		$16.00
Mrs. E. Etheridge	3 months		$4.00
Mrs. O'Birney	4 months		$12.00
Mrs. S. Turner	5 months		$19.00
Mrs. M. Turney	1 month		$4.00
Mrs. M. Shannon	4 months		$8.00
Mrs. M. McDonah	4 months		$16.00
Mrs. E. Parker	2 months		$6.00
Mrs. E. Woodley	2 months		$4.00
Mrs. M.A. Barber	4 months		$12.00
Mrs. C. Keter	2 months		$8.00
Mrs. Amey Mansfield	2 months		$4.00
Mrs. E. Woodley	2 months		$4.00
Mrs. E. Polk	2 months		$6.00
Mrs. Harrison	5 months		$15.00
Mrs. N. Garrett	1 month		$3.00
Mrs. A. Spaulding	3 months		$15.00
Mrs. M. Barber	1 month		$3.00
Mrs. E. Hudgins	1 month		$5.00
Mrs. R. Turner	1 month		$3.00
Mrs. Nainer	2 months		$6.00
Mrs. M. Mullin	2 months		$8.00
Mrs. B. King	2 months		$6.00
Mrs. S. Welsh	2 months		$6.00
Mrs. C. Harrington	2 months		$6.00
Mrs. Welsh	2 months		$6.00
Mrs. Dutton	2 months		$10.00
Mrs. Kennedy	2 months		$6.00
Mrs. Ed True	2 months		$10.00
Mrs. C. McDonah	1 month		$3.00
Mrs. Weston	2 months		$6.00
Mrs. Robins	2 months		$6.00
Mrs. Manning	3 months		$9.00
Mrs. Ann Stewart	2 months		$6.00
Mrs. Brummell	2 months		$4.00
Mrs. Guy	2 months		$6.00
Mrs. R. Wilder	2 months		$10.00

Mrs. Wood	2 months		$10.00
Mrs. E. Scarf	2 months		$6.00
Mrs. M. Elliott	2 months		$8.00
Mrs. C. Barber	5 months		$15.00
Mrs. West	2 months		$6.00
Mrs. Bounn	2 months		$8.00
Mrs. Birdsong	2 months		$6.00
Mrs. Barsoline	2 months		$8.00
Mrs. A. Boman	2 months		$8.00
Mrs. S. Butt	2 months		$10.00
Mrs. E. Hodges	2 months		$8.00
Mrs. H. Brown	2 months		$10.00
Mrs. Grey Beyton	2 months		$6.00
Mrs. E. Higgins	2 months		$6.00
Mrs. Smith	2 months		$5.00
Mrs. Clemmy	1 month		$6.00
Mrs. E. Stoakes	1 month		$2.00
Mrs. M. Halstead	1 month		$4.00
Mrs. Mellon	1 month		$3.00
Mrs. Parrish	1 month		$3.00
Mrs. Whitting	1 month		$5.00
Mrs. Curling	1 month		$4.00
Mrs. Richardson	1 month		$3.00

Report showing the number of inmates accommodated in the Norfolk County Parish House for the year ending 31 Mar 1858, the dates of admission and departure, how they were employed.

Alice Mansfield	6 Mar 1856		knitting
Sarah Saunders	4 Mar 1852		assisting the cook
Nancy Tally	8 Jul 1856		doing nothing
William Tally	27 May 1857	19 Jun 1857	
Polly Herd	4 Apr 1857		
James Waller	7 Apr 1857	8 Jun 1857	
John Parker	8 Apr 1857	died 18 Apr 1857	
James Barrington	9 Jun 1857	18 Jun 1857	
James Lewis	17 Jun 1857	26 Aug 1857	
Sarah Bass	18 Jul 1857	died 25 Jul 1857	
John R. James	12 Aug 1857	3 Sep 1857	
Mary Gwin	18 Aug 1857		
William T. Gwin	18 Aug 1857	going to school - small boy	
Jim Hall (slave)	16 Sep 1857		doing nothing
William P. Jordan	29 Sep 1857		idiot
Eliza Sykes	27 Sep 1857		cooking
Missouri Sykes	27 Sep 1857		small girl
Indiana Sykes	27 Sep 1857	27 Sep 1857	
Louisiana Sykes	27 Sep 1857	28 Sep 1857	
Frances Sykes	27 Sep 1857		small girl
Elijah Etheridge	6 Oct 1857	15 Oct 1857	

Patsey Cherry	16 Oct 1857	8 Jan 1858		
Isaiah Walker	26 Oct 1857	29 Oct 1857		
Mary Barnum	7 Jan 1857	23 May 1857		
Caroline Broughton	20 Jan 1857			
Mary Jane Broughton	20 Jan 1857			
Alexander McMullen	20 Nov 1857	31 Dec 1857		
Margaret Rayfield	28 Nov 1857		partially deranged	
Sarah Frances Rayfield	28 Nov 1857		small girl	
Mary Smith	2 Dec 1857			idiot
William P. Manning	27 Dec 1857			
Thomas Tatem (col)	31 Dec 1857	died 22 Jan 1859		
William Edgar	5 Jan 1858	30 Jan 1859		
Patrick H. Livington	8 Jan 1858	15 Mar 1859		
Elizabeth Evans	9 Jan 1858	died 10 Feb 1859		
Willoughby Dozier	16 Jan 1858			
James Liverman	20 Jan 1858	2 Mar 1858		
Catherine Bright	27 Feb 1858		doing nothing	
Ann Duncan	7 Feb 1857		knitting	
John Duncan	7 Feb 1857	going to school - small boy		
Dorothy Sparrow (col)	30 Mar 1857			blind
Daniel Sparrow (col)	30 Mar 1857	died 2 May 1857		
Thomas Brown	2 Jan 1857	died 18 Apr 1857		
John Flynn	20 Feb 1857	5 Jun 1857		
Harriet Woodward	2 Sep 1856	8 Oct 1857		
Mary Barnum	14 Nov 1857			
Emma Robertson & child Queen Elizabeth (colored)	18 Mar 1857	8 Jan 1858	went off without leave	
Joshua Hodges	6 Feb 1857	30 May 1858		
James Peed	5 Jan 1857	12 Aug 1858		

1858-1859 Entries

C - Tabular Statement for 1858 to 1859

Relating to Poor Persons assisted elsewhere than at the place of general reception.

(all are being assisted at home unless otherwise noted.)

NAME	LENGTH OF TIME, FROM & TO	Amount Contributed by overseer
Charles Everett	1 Jan to 1 Apr	$7.00
Nancy Cox	1 Apr to 1 Apr	$28.00
Polly Bonney	1 Apr to 1 Apr	$56.00
Sally Young	1 Dec to 1 Apr	$9.66
Harrison Johnson	1 Apr to 1 Apr	$34.00
Jim Elliott (col.)	1 Oct to 1 Apr	$12.00
Joseph M. Sikes	1 Apr to 1 Apr	$60.00
Henry Thompson	1 May to 1 Apr	$33.00
Elizabeth Fulford	1 Apr to 1 Jul	$15.00

Catharine Bright	1 Apr to 1 Apr	$28.00
J. Taylor	1 Jan to 1 Apr	$6.00
T. Halstead	1 Apr to 1 Apr	$24.00
Mrs. Cherry	1 Feb to 1 Apr	$4.00
Mrs. Stoakes	1 Oct to 1 Feb	$8.00
Isaac Young (col.)	1 Jan to 1 Mar	$4.00
David King	1 Jan to 1 Apr	$6.50
Elvin Cherry	1 Oct to 1 Apr	$11.95
Mrs. Turner	1 Feb to 1 Apr	$4.00
James Watts (col.)	1 Mar to 1 Apr	$3.00
P. Kazer	1 Mar to 1 Apr	$3.00
A. Hardy	1 Mar to 1 Apr	$2.00

Statement C for Overseers of the Poor 17 May 1858

Report showing the number of inmates accommodated in the Norfolk County Parish House during the year ending 31 Mar 1859, the date of those admitted and departed during the year and how they are employed

NAME	WHEN ADMITTED	WHEN LEFT	HOW EMPLOYED	REMARKS
Alice Mansfield	6 Mar 1856		knitting	
Polly Herd	4 Apr 1857		knitting	
Sarah Sanders	4 Mar 1852		helping the cook	
Dorita Sparrow	30 Mar 1857	died 3 Mar 1859		free colored
James Hall	16 Sep 1857		doing nothing	
Mary Barnum	14 Nov 1857		helping the cook	
Nancy Tally	8 Jul 1856	16 Apr 1858	doing nothing	
William Jordan	19 Sep 1857		doing nothing - idiot	
Mary Gwin & son William	18 Aug 1857	6 May 1858	doing nothing	
Polly Smith	2 Dec 1857	died 24 Apr 1858		
Caroline Broughton	20 Nov 1857		knitting	
Margaret Baysfield	28 Nov 1857		doing nothing - partially deranged	
child Sarah Frances	born 10 Dec 1858			
Ann Duncan	7 Feb 1857	29 Jul 1858		
son John Duncan		24 May 1858[24]		
William P. Manning	27 Dec 1857	24 Jul 1858		
Willoughby Dozier	16 Jan 1858	26 Jul 1858		
William P. Manning	27 Dec 1858			
Kizziah Dyer & son John	21 Oct 1858			
Alfreda the dau of Kizziah Dyer	born 20 Feb 1859			
Artzenia Bailey	2 Sep 1858	21 Oct 1858		
Catherine Bright	27 Feb 1858		doing nothing - deformed & dumb	

[24] It's illogical that a mother moved out of the poor house before her son, but he might have been apprenticed and therefore moved out of the poor house. There is no additional info in this record.

Arthur Creekmur	8 Apr 1858	died 24 Apr 1858	doing nothing	
Wilson Creekmur	6 Sep 1858	12 Nov 1858	doing nothing	
Emmy Robinson & child Elizabeth	28 May 1858		sewing at times - partially deranged, Negro	
Williard Jones	25 Oct 1858	died 12 Nov 1858		
John Daniels	3 Feb 1859	died 27 Feb 1859		
James Swain[25]	27 Nov 1858	22 Mar 1859		
John Welsh	15 Feb 1859			
Janet Smith	14 Mar 1859			free colored

David Lynch, Keeper

SCHEDULE B

Report showing the number of Inmates accommodated in the Norfolk County Alms House during the year ending 31 Mar 1860, the date of those admitted and departed during the year and how they are employed.

NAME	WHEN ADMITTED	WHEN LEFT	HOW EMPLOYED	REMARKS
William P. Manning	26 Jul 1859	26 Jan 1860		
John Minton	1 Aug 1859	17 Jan 1860		
John Dyer	10 Oct 1859	28 Jan 1860	taken home with Josephus Roach - small boy	
Kizia Dyer & child	10 Oct 1859	2 Mar 1860		
Alfreda Dyer	10 Oct 1859	2 Mar 1860		child
Patsey Cherry	15 Oct 1859		knitting when able - under the doctor's hands	
John P. Dornenburg	8 Nov 1859	died 16 Dec 1860		
Robert R. King	14 Sep 1859		doing nothing - chronic rheumatism	
Mary Minton & 5 children	1 Aug 1859		knitting & nursing children	
Benjamin Minton	1 Aug 1859	1 Jan 1860		
Isiah Minton	1 Aug 1859		going to school	boy
Martha Minton	1 Aug 1859			small girl
1 with no name 8 years old	1 Aug 1859			small girl
Catherine Bright	27 Feb 1858		deformed & dumb	
Eliza Sikes & 2 children	27 Sep 1857		cooking & washing	
Missouri Sikes	27 Sep 1857		going to school	small girl
Frances Sikes	27 Sep 1857		going to school	small girl
Jim Hall (colored)	16 Sep 1857	died 25 Oct 1859		colored slave

---

[25] This one is a "best guess" based on the handwriting. It looks like which as you can tell is not legible enough.

James Liverman	20 Jan 1858	29 Aug 1859	
John Welsh	15 Feb 1859	30 Jul 1859	
Janet Smith (col.)	14 Mar 1859	died 14 Apr 1859	free colored
Polly Herd	4 Apr 1857	died 20 Jun 1859	
Margaret Rayfield	28 Nov 1857		deranged
Alice Mansfield	1 Jun 1856	20 Jun 1859	transferred to Portsmouth Parish Alms House
Caroline Broughton	20 Nov 1857	20 Jun 1859	transferred to Portsmouth Parish Alms House
Sarah Sanders	4 Mar 1852	20 Jun 1859	transferred to Portsmouth Parish Alms House
William Jourdon	19 Sep 1857	20 Jun 1859	transferred to Portsmouth Parish Alms House
Emey Robertson & child (colored)	28 May 1858	20 Jun 1859	transferred to Portsmouth Parish Alms House
Queen Robertson (colored)	28 May 1858	20 Jun 1859	transferred to Portsmouth Parish Alms House

1859-1860 Entries

Motion made on behalf of Wright Archer by Timothy Cuffee, his next friend.

Notice to Horatio Creekmur to appear at the next term of this Court to show cause why the order passed at February term authorizing the Overseers of the Poor to bind Wright, a free Negro, son of Annis Archer, to him should not be revoked on the ground that the said order was improperly granted.
Filed 24 Feb 1860

SCHEDULE C

Tabular Statement Relating to Poor Persons assisted elsewhere than at place of general reception 1859-1860. *(Note "at home" is applicable to all of the entries unless otherwise noted)*

NAME	LENGTH OF TIME			
Henry Thompson	1 Apr 1859	31 Mar 1860		$36.00
Isaac Young	1 Apr 1859	31 Mar 1860		$24.00
Mrs. Stokes	1 Apr 1859	31 Jul 1859		$6.00
James Watts	1 Apr 1859	31 Mar 1860		$44.50
Amelia Hardy	1 Apr 1859	31 Mar 1860		$30.50
David King	1 Dec 1859	28 Feb 1860		$5.00
Nancy Cox	1 Apr 1859	31 Mar 1860		$22.00
Ann King	1 Apr 1859	31 Mar 1860		$20.00
Serepta Nichols	one month			$3.00
Susanna Turner	1 Apr 1859	31 Mar 1860		$36.00
Harrison Johnson	1 Apr 1859	31 Mar 1860		$36.00
James Elliott	1 Apr 1859	31 Mar 1860		$36.00
Joseph M. Sikes	1 Apr 1859	31 Mar 1860	T.W. Sikes	$75.00
Elizabeth Hodges & 2 children	1 Apr 1859	31 Mar 1860		$36.00
Thomas Graham	1 Apr 1859	31 Mar 1860		$24.00

Polly Bonney	1 Apr 1859	31 Mar 1860		$30.16
Mrs. Stringer	1 Apr 1859	31 May 1859		$6.00
Elizabeth Halstead & 3 children	1 Dec 1859	1 Dec 1859		$10.00
Elizabeth Sikes & 2 children	1 Dec 1859	1 Dec 1859		$9.00

1867-1868 Entries

The Overseers of the Poor of Norfolk County respectfully report to the Court of said County that during the fiscal year ending 31 Mar 1868 they have supported at the place of general reception 28 persons, 19 of whom were white and 9 colored and at other places 10 persons, 9 of whom were white and 1 colored. Making in all 38 persons, 28 of whom were white and 10 colored. Their names are as follows to wit:

Margaret Baysfield	Azena Bailey
Samuel Scott	Walter DeLastation
Eliza Cox	Rosa Ann Martin
William T. Cox	Mary Thomas
Mary Dunford	James Holstead
Richard Turner	Eldustus Mooney
Elizabeth Foreman	Margaret Mooney
John Foreman	Eliza Mooney
Rebecca Turner	Madora Thomas
Mary F. Miller	
Colored	Colored
Mary Hancock	Nancy Briggs
Jesse Wilkins	Henry Briggs
Ishorne Wright	John Briggs
Jessie Porter	Ann Briggs
John Wilson	

At other places than that of general reception.

Sarah O'Brien	A.M. Weston
Mrs. White	Fanny Richard
Mr. White	Joseph M. Sikes
Mrs. Taylor	Mrs. Hudgins
Mrs. Snail	
Colored	America

The expenses for the maintenance of the whole including contingent expenses was $1,817, $1,627 for support of those at the place of general reception and $190 for those at other places.

They have received from the Sheriff $1,500 dollars of the $4000 dollars required for the past year which leaves a balance of $2,500 due to the Overseers from the levy of 1867.

They recommend that the Court make the levy for the present year 1868, so as to raise for the support of the poor for the current year $2,000 dollars and for payments of old debt and interest thereon $3,500 for a total of $5,500

If the Court shall find that any part of the $2,500 dollars remaining unpaid out of the levy for 1867 can now be made available it will lessen the amount now required by the poor.

Thomas Brown
President

This is a list of those at Poor House (white and colored) as well as how long each has been provided for during this year.

Name	Time Provided for	
Robert King	one year	sick
Catharine Bright	one year	deformed and dumb
Margaret Baysfield	one year	deranged
Patsey Cherry	6 months	doing nothing (unable)
Arzena Bailey	6 months	doing nothing (unable)
James Liverman	3 months	gardening
John Minton	2 months	unable to do anything
Mary Minton	2 months	unable to do anything
Isaiah Minton	2 months	unable to do anything
Martha Minton	2 months	unable to do anything
Benjamin Minton	2 months	unable to do anything
Virginia Minton	2 months	unable to do anything
William Cuffee (colored)	9 months	unable to do anything
George Sikes	1 month	unable to do anything
Henry P. Gwinn	3 months	unable to do anything
Thomas Burke	2 months	unable to do anything
Mary Miller	1 month	unable to do anything
Lucinda Hewlett	1 month	unable to do anything
Eliza Sikes	one year	cooking and washing
Missouri Sikes	one year	at school
Frances Sikes	one year	at school
Henry Thompson	one year	
----- Graham	one year	
----- Elliott	one year	
----- Johnson	one year	
J. Watts	one year	
A. Hardy	one year	
M. Yore	1 month	
S. Cherry	one year	

A. King	one year	
N. Cox	one year	
J.W. Sikes	one year	
E. Hodges	one year	
E. Halstead	one year	
S. Turner	one year	
Miles Newman	one year	
B.T. Strange	1 month	
C.R. Fisher	1 month	
T. Keeler	one year	

Total amount received by the overseers for the year.
Amount from Annual Levy: $1,976.19
Amount received from all sources other than levy: $459.44

Total amount expended by the overseers within the year, as well at place of general reception as elsewhere.
At place of general reception: $1,334.77
At other places other than general reception $813.14

Balance in hands of overseers if any: $149.14
Amount required to pay arrears (if any) of the past year and expenditures of the ensuing year $2,000.00
The Board of Overseers recommend that the Court make the levy for the year at 60 cents per tythe or head
T.H. Brown
President

1888 ENTRIES

21 May 1888
To the Hon. George D. Parker, Judge Norfolk County Court:
We the undersigned earnestly petition your Honor, to appoint Mr. Samuel J. Nichols, Sr. to succeed Mr. F. Hanbury (deceased) in the office of Overseer of the Poor in Pleasant Grove District.

We know Mr. Nichols to be a suitable man for the position as well as the choice of our people.

Respectfully *[signed]* G.A. Wilson, J.N. Eason, LeRoy M. Nicholas, William T. Gammon, C.D. Woodward, C.C. Jackson, J.A. Stout, E.C. Hall, R.A. Hall, Wesley Hall, J.S. Hall, William Smith, John Lokhart *[Lockhart]*, Albert P. Old

UNKNOWN DATE
We the Jury find for the plaintiff £6.5.4 half penny.
[signed] John Lee

Captain Field, Merchant Taylor, at Portsmouth, recommended by Joseph Morse.

INDEX

www.ingramcontent.com/pod-product-compliance
Lightning Source LLC
LaVergne TN
LVHW061248100826
845148LV00008B/1058

* 9 7 8 0 7 8 8 4 2 9 6 5 1 *